'In these days, Nicholson would probably have risen to greater eminence. During the period when he lived he knew the world was chiefly alive to the progress of mind and political science – now the external universe obtains far more consideration. As a man of invention, of acquirement – of mingled theory and practice – Nicholson would have prospered in these days of mines, tunnels, railroad and steam engines.'

— Mary Shelley, *Life of William Godwin*, c.1836-40, Bodleian Libraries, University of Oxford, MS. Abinger c.60.

THE LIFE OF
WILLIAM NICHOLSON,
1753-1815

A Memoir of Enlightenment Commerce, Politics, Arts and Science
Written by his son William Nicholson, in 1868

Edited by
SUE DURRELL

Afterword by
Frank A.J.L. James, Professor of the History of Science,
the Royal Institution and University College London

PETER OWEN PUBLISHERS
London and Chicago

First published in Great Britain 2018 by Peter Owen Publishers

PETER OWEN PUBLISHERS
Conway Hall, 25 Red Lion Square, London WC1R 4RL
peterowen.com

Peter Owen books are distributed in the USA and Canada by
Independent Publishers Group/Trafalgar Square
814 North Franklin Street, Chicago, IL, 60610, USA

ISBN 978-0-7206-1957-7
A catalogue record for this book is available from the British Library.
Printed and bound in the UK by CPI

To Andy, Matt and Jonathan.
You mean the world to me.

CONTENTS

EDITOR'S INTRODUCTION

This is the first publication of a handwritten memoir by the son of the natural philosopher, inventor and editor William Nicholson. It was written 150 years ago, in 1868. For the last forty years, this document has been available only to scholars of the Enlightenment visiting the Bodleian Library at the University of Oxford.

William Nicholson (1753–1815) lived at a time when life was not separated into different disciplines for the ease of marketing. He was free to explore wherever his interests lay, without worrying about the impact a lack of specialization might have upon his career, at a time when the secrets of life were unfolding with increasing rapidity.

An inquisitive, ingenious and hard-working young man, his quest for enlightenment knew no boundaries and thus extended across navigation and horology, publishing and printing, the literary and creative arts, natural philosophy and electricity, mathematics and naval architecture, technology and patents, manufacturing and civil engineering.

I first became aware of the existence of Nicholson through the master potter Josiah Wedgwood (1730–1795). In 1984 an award-winning museum and visitor centre opened on the site of the Wedgwood factory in Barlaston, a leafy village to the south of Stoke-on-Trent, not far from my home. In 2009, exactly 250 years after it was established, the Wedgwood business had fallen victim to cheap imports from the Far East, the recession and weak management. One financial problem after another led to Staffordshire's (and arguably the UK's) best-known manufacturing business going into receivership with a £134 million hole in the company pension fund. For several years, it appeared that nearly £18 million of this liability would fall on the tiny shoulders of the museum trust whose only means of clearing the debt would be to sell the Wedgwood collection, potentially dispersing it in the process.

Miraculously, this was resolved in 2014 when the collection was transferred to the Victoria and Albert Museum following a major appeal by the Heritage Lottery Fund, the National Art Fund and the support of Staffordshire telecoms entrepreneur John Caudwell, together with many private supporters.

The financial problems at Wedgwood were much in the media in 2009, when my son was given a homework project to create a family tree. My mother provided one for her side of the family which started with 'William Nicholson (1753–1815)' and a few scant details including the dates of two voyages to China and the note '1777 agent for Josiah Wedgwood, Amsterdam'. Fearing that the Wedgwood archives might not be on my doorstep for much longer, I made an appointment to see what Nicholson might have been doing with Wedgwood in the Netherlands.

Equipped with my white cotton gloves, I was delighted to find a veritable treasure trove of documentation from between 1775 and 1777 comprising a series of letters and accounts handwritten by Nicholson to Wedgwood and his business partner Thomas Bentley. This correspondence details how Nicholson successfully negotiated the transfer of Wedgwood's Dutch agency from the incompetent Cooper and Du Burk to the very successful Lambertus van Veldhuysen, with Josiah Wedgwood writing to Thomas Bentley in 1777: 'I have not the least doubt of Mr Nicholson's integrity and honour.'[1]

Aside from his work for the pottery business in Amsterdam, I came away with two further lines of enquiry linking Nicholson and Wedgwood.

First, they were both members of the coffee house philosophical society established by Richard Kirwan in 1780. This society comprised

---

1.   E18774-25, V&A/Wedgwood Collection, 1777.

some of the most eminent and progressive men of the late eighteenth century including members of the Midlands-based Lunar Society: Joseph Priestley, James Watt, Matthew Boulton and John Whitehurst. Other members included Jean-Hyacinthe de Magellan, Adair Crawford and William Babington; Nicholson performed the role of secretary alongside Babington from 1784. Rather inconveniently, Kirwan did not want this society to have a name – although in this memoir it is referred to as the Chapter Coffee House Society after the location of its inaugural meeting.

Second, Nicholson also served as secretary to Wedgwood in 1785 when the latter was chairman of the General Chamber of Manufacturers. Nicholson collated and published the evidence of numerous manufacturers for an inquiry before the Committee of the House of Lords relating to the proposed trade treaty with Ireland. This exercise introduced him to many of Britain's leading industrialists who were struggling with problems of cheap imports, export restrictions, industrial espionage and infringement of their intellectual property – *plus ça change!*

I have always been interested in industrial heritage, and for a time I was involved with museums via the charity Arts & Business, so the prospect of a direct connection with so many historic figures made me hungry for more information. I was then reminded of an ancestor's ship's log[2] from a voyage with the East India Company to China in the early 1770s. This was in the possession of my uncle, who had a drawer of papers relating to my great-great-great-great-great-grandfather William Nicholson.

This collection included a copy of *The Life of William Nicholson by His Son William*[3], a memoir that William Nicholson Junior (1789–1874) had written in 1868, when he was eighty years old. His memories of his father, his home life, his father's friends and associates – 'among the most distinguished philosophers of those days' – are vivid and frequently charming.

---

2. William Nicholson, *Ship's Log for* The Gatton, *From England towards Canton*, 1772–3.

3. MSS. Don. d. 175, e. 125, Bodleian Library at the University of Oxford.

More familiar names emerged from the memoir, including the dramatist Thomas Holcroft; the political activists William Godwin, Mary Wollstonecraft and John Thelwall; the liberal publishers Joseph Johnson and George Robinson; artists such as John Bacon and James Barry; industrialists Richard Trevithick and Jabez Hornblower; doctors Sir Anthony Carlisle, Charles Combe and William Buchan; scientists Alessandro Volta, Sir Humphry Davy, Sir Joseph Banks, Count Rumford and Friedrich Accum; nobility such as Baron Camelford II, Lord Middleton, the Earl of Dundonald and Earl Stanhope. This was an extraordinary network for any man.

Aside from Nicholson's administrative work he also managed to build a healthy income from writing. His first successful publication was *An Introduction to Natural Philosophy* in 1782, and he went on to publish numerous works on navigation, historic biographies and scientific translations. His greatest legacy was *A Journal of Natural Philosophy, Chemistry and the Arts*, which he launched in 1797 and edited monthly until 1813. (See APPENDIX A for a full list of his published works.)

He was also an inventor, designing a hydrometer (a device that measures the specific gravity of solids); a compact scale rule (as an alternative to Gunther's rule, the standard used in navigation); the revolving doubler (the first automatic rotating machine built to generate electricity by influence); the cylinder printing machine (the first design of a rotary printer, later commercialized by Friedrich Koenig); an innovative gravity escapement clock; a file manufacturing machine; and a device for producing a blast of steam for chemical or engineering purposes. (See APPENDIX B for details of his inventions.)

Having registered four patents, Nicholson went on to help others, such as Richard Trevithick, with their patent applications. He was called as an expert witness in one of the most important patent cases of the time, Matthew Boulton's and James Watt's claim of patent infringement against Jabez Hornblower and John Maberly in 1796.

With so many avenues of research to pursue, it was easy to keep putting all Nicholson's electro-chemical activities (the aspect that excited me least, I confess) to one side, especially as I was not even thinking of writing a book.

Fortunately I discovered Professor Hasok Chang who, while at University College London, had launched an online *Virtual Nicholson's Journal* to enhance his students' understanding of primary sources in the history of science. A huge fan of Nicholson, describing him as a 'neglected figure' and 'in need of a biography', Professor Chang was extremely generous in helping me to understand the history of the science behind the decomposition of water, particularly the significance of an article by Nicholson about the torpedo fish, which had provided Alessandro Volta with an important clue in the construction of his pile. This was acknowledged by Volta in his letter to Sir Joseph Banks in 1800, in which he commented, 'The hypothesis of this learned and laborious philosopher . . . is indeed very ingenious.'[4]

In May 1800, it was with a copy of Volta's pile (battery) that Nicholson and his friend Anthony Carlisle decomposed water at number 10 Soho Square – a discovery praised by Humphry Davy, who enthused that 'an immense field of investigation seems opened by this discovery: may it be pursued so as to acquaint us with some of the laws of life!'[5]

I was beginning to wonder whom Nicholson had not met? The list of his friends and acquaintances reads like a Who's Who of the second half of the eighteenth century. The screenwriter William Nicholson (who kindly responded to an email of mine) speculated whether he might even be a fictional character like William Boyd's

---

4. Alessandro Volta, 'The Electricity Excited by the Mere Contact of Conducting Substances of Different Kinds'. In a letter from Mr Alexander Volta, FRS Professor of Natural Philosophy in the University of Pavia, to the Rt Hon. Sir Joseph Banks, Bart KB, PRS, *Philosophical Transactions of the Royal Society*, Vol. 90, 1800.

5. Humphry Davy to Davies Giddy, 3 July 1800, John Ayrton Paris, *The Life of Sir Humphry Davy* (2 volumes, London, 1831), Vol. I, pp. 85–8.

Logan Mountstuart, and I was reminded of Forrest Gump.[6]

I could not help but wonder why someone with so many important connections, who contributed not a little to science and manufacturing and who left behind such a prolific body of work was so little known.

There is no shortage of materials. The great essayist William Hazlitt, who was asked by Nicholson and Godwin to complete Holcroft's biography, compared their output:

> *I used to write a page or two perhaps in half a year, and I remember laughing heartily at the celebrated experimentalist Nicholson who told me that in twenty years he had written as much as would make three hundred octavo volumes.*[7]

Increasingly curious, in my spare time I pursued various lines of research into Nicholson's activities, and it became apparent that each expert only knew Nicholson for only one or two of his activities – no one seemed to fully appreciate the myriad activities in which Nicholson had been involved. The print historians knew about the publishing, but not the seafaring and slide rules. The horologists knew about the clock, but not the literary connections. The economists knew about Wedgwood but not the civil engineering. The scientists were not aware of his commercial activities.

By 2012 I had managed to amass a substantial amount of material on Nicholson. Although my family was not entirely persuaded by the merits of my growing obsession, it was becoming clear that if a biography of Nicholson were to be written it seemed that I had the best collection of material for such a task. When Hasok Chang, the Hans Rausing Professor of History and Philosophy of Science at the

---

6. Fictional characters who met famous characters from history: Logan Mountstuart, in *Any Human Heart* by William Boyd, met Virginia Woolf, Evelyn Waugh, Ernest Hemingway and James Joyce. Forrest Gump, in the film inspired by the novel of the same name by Winston Groom, met Elvis Presley, John Lennonand three US presidents.

7. William Hazlitt, *Table-talk: or Original Essays*, London: J. Warren, 1821.

University of Cambridge and former president of the British History of Science, told me it was 'much needed', who was I to argue?

It is worth noting that while Nicholson is currently best known among historians of science, I'm not aware that he ever called himself a man of science – he referred to himself as a natural philosopher, a journalist, a mechanic, a patent agent and lastly as a civil engineer. While his scientific reputation rests on the launch of his *Journal* in 1797 and his work on the decomposition of water in 1800, he was forty-four when he launched his journal and had already been busy and productive for a quarter of a century in commercial and literary activities.

With 2015 marking the 200th anniversary of Nicholson's death I naïvely thought (ever the optimist) that this might be an ideal year to aim towards for publishing a biography. I did manage to launch a website – *www.nicholsonsjournal.com* – on the bicentenary of Nicholson's death in May 2015. This allows historians to search the titles of all 2,860 articles published in the *Journal*. It was described in the *Guardian* as 'not only a useful online tool, but also a valuable reminder that there is another kind of historical scientific journal than the Philosophical Transactions, waiting for exploration'.[8]

However, the biography is taking much longer to complete, as the answer to one question always reveals more lines of inquiry and other people to consult, especially as Nicholson's interests were so wide ranging and he appears to have been such a workaholic. In particular, there is still much to uncover about Nicholson's work as a civil engineer after 1808, when he was involved at the waterworks in Hammersmith, Portsmouth, Southwark and the Regent's Canal.

Having made substantial progress (110,000 words at the time of writing) it was becoming a challenge to decide how to incorporate

---

8. Anna Gielas, 'Nicholson's Journal: Britain's first commercial science periodical' in *The H Word Blog* for the *Guardian*, 8 March 2016, *www.theguardian.com/science/the-h-word/2016/mar/08/nicholsons-journal-britains-first-commercial-science-periodical* (accessed 19 December 2017).

The Life of William Nicholson by His Son William within the broader narrative. Some of the information is taken from family papers or newspaper articles published during Nicholson's life or shortly afterwards, while much of it comprises the son's personal recollections and vivid sketches of life in the Nicholson family. And, of course, William Nicholson Junior knew very little about his father's life before he was born and after he left home in 1808.

The chronology of this memoir is often not sequential, and several recollections do not include Nicholson. Nevertheless, they relate to amusing and colourful experiences that young William had with associates of his father, such as the surgeon Anthony Carlisle and Jack Sadler, a chemical assistant to Humphry Davy at the Royal Institution, where Nicholson was appointed to the Committee for Chemical Investigation and Analysis. While it would seem logical to exclude the unrelated passages from Nicholson's biography, I was conscious that this would leave some interesting stories unpublished – stories that might be a missing piece in another historian's jigsaw puzzle.

Variety was very much the spice of Nicholson family life, and father and son were both captivated by the connections between science and the arts, telling of trips to now-famous artists and how scientific discoveries were used to create special effects in the theatres of London. This memoir provides the reader with a window on to a fascinating cross-section of Georgian life at the heart of the Enlightenment.

While the modern biography of William Nicholson (1753–1815) is still in progress, awareness of Nicholson's work is growing – he now has his own Twitter account @Wm_Nicholson.

Given the increasing awareness of and interest in our protagonist, it seemed sensible to publish, as an *amuse-bouche*, this short memoir of William Nicholson, 150 years after it was written in 1868.

For anyone with an interest in Georgian life, this provides a very intimate and enjoyable account of some of the best-known personalities of the Enlightenment, as well as glimpses into the life of a large family of that period.

Just as through his *Journal* Nicholson enjoyed encountering men of 'talent and virtue', I have been lucky enough to meet or correspond with eminent historians of science, literature, business, publishing, horology, civil engineering and art. I have been touched by the number of experts who have generously shared their time, their knowledge and their advice in recognition and respect of Nicholson's many contributions and a desire that he should be better known.

I hope that this memoir sparks more interest in William Nicholson, a man who was 'regardless of fame'[9] and whose great desire was always to be useful, as indeed he was. I hope that you will enjoy discovering him.

---

9. *The European Magazine, and London Review*, Vol. 62, 1812.

ACKNOWLEDGEMENTS

A big thank you to my Uncle Nick for lending me all the manuscripts and my mother Patricia for looking after the 1789 paper – we will uncover its significance one day!

Most particularly, I would like to express my heartfelt gratitude to Katie Foster, Hasok Chang, Hugh Torrens, Frank James and Anthony Francis-Jones who have been so generous in helping me understand the historical and scientific context for Nicholson's life and inventions. My appreciation also goes to Iain Watts, Jonathan Betts MBE, Joyce Townsend, Jerry Bentley, Pamela Hunter, Rupert Baker, Len Barnett, Pamela Clemit, Rod Home and Timoer Frelink who have provided invaluable input that will be more evident in the modern biography.

Special thanks go to Natasha Chare and Kelly Buckley, who ploughed through the indexes of Nicholson's *Journals* to help create the online database, as well as to Ruth Millington, Freddie Wildblood, Pauline Chare, Alice Mackey and Pamela Skipwith who helped with research and proofing.

Thank you to the team at Exesios, who designed and built the website *www.nicholsonsjournal.com* and designed this book cover, and to everyone at Peter Owen for helping to finish a job started 150 years ago in 1868 – especially for agreeing to the footnotes!

ILLUSTRATIONS

Inside front cover

'Drew's New and Correct Plan of the Cities of London and Westminster, the Borough of Southwark &C.' Published by J. Drew, 1786. Private collection.

Page 35

Portrait of William Nicholson (1753–1815), stipple engraving by Thomas Blood for the *European Magazine*, after an original painting by Samuel Drummond A.R.A (whereabouts of original are unknown). Published by J. Asperne, Cornhill, 1 September 1812. Private collection.

Inside back cover

Illustration accompanying Patent GB1748 of 1790 to William Nicholson of New North Street, Red Lion Square, Middlesex: 'A Machine or Instrument on a New Construction for the Purpose of Printing on Paper, Linen, Cotton, Woollen and Other Articles in a More Neat, Cheap and Accurate Manner Than Is Effected by the Machines Now in Use'. Private collection.

ILLUSTRATIONS

EDITORIAL NOTE I

The manuscript

The manuscript papers by William Nicholson Junior, now in the Bodleian, include several drafts of some sections, and consequently I have included the best of both where versions differed. Factual and typographical mistakes made by William the son have been corrected silently, with any significant errors referenced in the notes. Any remaining mistakes are entirely mine. The original manuscript is held by the Bodleian Library at the University of Oxford (MSS. Don. d. 175, e. 125).

EDITORIAL NOTE II

The author, William Nicholson Junior (1789–1874)

One of twelve children, at least ten of whom survived to adulthood, William was the oldest son of William and Catherine Nicholson. After playing 'war with the French' at school, he would return home to be roped into helping with an experiment or to run an errand to one of his father's associates. He was free to explore the 'Eldorados' of workshops, theatres, artists' studios, hospitals and even military grounds with few restrictions, overhearing conversations about politics, espionage, the arts and natural philosophy.

In his late teens he accompanied his father to help with surveying on civil engineering projects for a few years, before leaving to work for Lord Middleton at his Birdsall Estates in Malton, Yorkshire. Here, he met and married his wife, Rebecca Brown, in August 1815. They had a son, John Lee Nicholson, in 1817, and a daughter, Jane, in 1826. By 1828 Nicholson had moved to Manchester, where he built a career as a land agent and civil engineer. From 1835 he took on work as a patent agent, following in his father's footsteps.

William wrote this memoir of his father between 1868 and 1869, and looking back some sixty years he clearly has fond memories of his indulgent parents and the warm and interesting home in which he was raised. He takes great pride in his father's polymathic accomplishments and wishes to set the matter straight on a few injustices, as he sees them. Although he is clearly biased (failing to mention Nicholson's debt problems), I'd like to think we can forgive a son such loyalty to his father and the few inaccuracies that any of us might make when we reach our eighties. We can be grateful that he decided to 'put down the things that I have seen only'.

Rebecca died in 1869 and William moved to Hull to be near to their son, who was a surgeon. By 1871 William was living alone in Sculcoates and is recorded in the census as a 'retired engineer'. He died in 1874.

EDITORIAL NOTE III

The afterword

Young William seems distinctly less interested in science than his father, and so historians of science and scientific communications may, like Iain Watts in his award-winning paper on scientific publishing,[10] find that the 'manuscript is less helpful than one might

---

10. Iain P. Watts,'"We Want No Authors": William Nicholson and the Contested Role of the Scientific Journal in Britain, 1797–1813', *British Journal for the History of Science*, 2014, Vol. 47, pp. 397–419.

expect'. Much is missing from the memoir regarding Nicholson's scientific achievements, yet his contribution to the improvement in scientific communications in Britain was so important that I felt this could not be consigned to mere footnotes.

I am therefore delighted to include an afterword written by Frank A. J. L. James to accompany this memoir, particularly as it traces a direct line to Nicholson's involvement at the Royal Institution and to University College London, which holds one of the earliest examinations of Nicholson's work.[11]

The afterword, 'Locating William Nicholson', places Nicholson's 'critically important contributions' in the context of revolutionary Enlightenment in science, politics, the arts and communications and posits one theory as to why Nicholson was never made a fellow of the Royal Society and therefore is not as well known as he might be.

Sue Durrell, 2018

---

11. Roy Woolner, *The Life and Scientific Work of William Nicholson 1753–1815*, London: University of London, 1959.

TIMELINE FOR THE LIFETIME OF WILLIAM NICHOLSON (1753–1815)

See APPENDIX A for full list of Nicholson's publications.

Items marked with * have not been confirmed.

Year	Nicholson's home and family	Nicholson's employment, inventions, patents	Nicholson's world
1752			Benjamin Franklin attempts to collect electricity from lightning
1753	William Nicholson is born 13 December, Great Carter Lane, London		British Museum opens
1754	Baptism at St Pancras Old Church		The Marriage Act comes into force, requiring a formal ceremony
1755			Samuel Johnson's *A Dictionary of the English Language* is published. Joseph Black discovers fixed air (carbon dioxide).
1756			Start of the Seven Years War (1756–1763)
1757			William Blake and Agnes Ibbetson are born
1758			Work starts on the Bridgewater Canal
1759			Josiah Wedgwood's business founded in Staffordshire
1760	Catherine Bouillie is born 24 March, Warwick Street, London		King George II dies, and George III becomes King
1761			Matthew Boulton opens the Soho Manufactory in Birmingham

Year	Nicholson's home and family	Nicholson's employment, inventions, patents	Nicholson's world
1762	William goes to school near Richmond, Yorkshire		Voltaire argues for separation of church and state
1763			End of the Seven Years War (1756–1763)
1764			James Hargreaves invents the spinning jenny
1765			The Stamp Act is passed, imposing a tax on printed materials
1766			First Anglo-Mysore war starts (1767–1769). Henry Cavendish recognizes hydrogen gas as 'inflammable air'.
1767			Joseph Priestley publishes the *History and Present State of Electricity*
1768	Leaves school to join the East India Company	First voyage to China	Captain Cook sails to the South Pacific in *Endeavour*
1769			James Watt's first patent for steam engine granted
1770			Captain Cook lands in Australia
1771			Smeatonian Society of Civil Engineers founded. Carl Wilhelm Scheele discovers gas later named oxygen.
1772		Midshipman on *The Gatton* to China	Lord Mansfield rules for the slave James Somersett that 'no slave could be forcibly removed from Britain and sold into slavery'
1773		Returns from China	The Tea Act is passed in May, and the Boston Tea Party occurs in December

Year	Nicholson's home and family	Nicholson's employment, inventions, patents	Nicholson's world
1774		* Teaching mathematics in Wakefield	Joseph Priestley publishes his discovery of the gas later named oxygen
1775		* Employed in attorney's office in Chelsea. First visit to Amsterdam for Wedgwood.	Start of American Revolutionary War (1775–1783). J.M.W. Turner is born.
1776			Adam Smith publishes *The Wealth of Nations*. Watt's steam engine is produced. Declaration of Independence by thirteen of the North American colonies.
1777	Living in Amsterdam. Returns to London (October).	Commercial agent for Wedgwood in Amsterdam	Sheridan's *The School for Scandal* is performed at the Theatre Royal
1778	Lodging with Holcroft in Southampton Row		Antoine Lavoisier recognizes and names oxygen. Voltaire dies.
1779			Samuel Crompton invents the spinning mule
1780		Philosophical society established by Richard Kirwan in Chapter Coffee House	Luigi Galvani identifies electrical charge in living tissues
1781	Marries Catherine Bouillie (4 October) at St Giles, Holborn		World's first Iron Bridge opens in Shropshire
1782	Living Warwick Street, Golden Square. Sarah Nicholson born (21 February).	Holcroft's *Duplicity* performed at Theatre Royal	Montgolfier Brothers test flight of a hot-air balloon. Josiah Wedgwood's paper on his pyrometer read to the Royal Society.
1783	Living at 33 Oxford Street	Joins Richard Kirwan's philosophical society	End of the American Revolutionary War (1775–1783)

Year	Nicholson's home and family	Nicholson's employment, inventions, patents	Nicholson's world
1784	Anne Nicholson born (20 April)	Invention of hydrometer. Elected joint secretary of philosophical society.	Henry Cavendish outlines the composition of water in his Royal Society paper 'Experiments on Air'
1785		Becomes secretary of the General Chamber of Manufacturers	Sarah Siddons makes début as Lady Macbeth at Theatre Royal
1786		Invention of scale rule and submission to the Board of Longitude	Caroline Herschel discovers the first of eight comets
1787	* Robert Nicholson born. Mary Nicholson born (28 November)	General Chamber of Manufacturers folds	Society for the Abolition of the Slave Trade is founded, and Josiah Wedgwood produces anti-slavery medallion
1788		Invention of revolving doubler	Linnean Society of London is established
1789	Living at 27 New North Street. William Nicholson born (31 October)		Fall of the Bastille in Paris. French Revolution begins (1789–99).
1790		Patent 1748: cylindrical printing machine. Executor to J. H. Magellan.	Edmund Burke publishes *Reflections on the Revolution in France*. Mary Wollstonecraft publishes *A Vindication of the Rights of Man*
1791	* John Nicholson born	Establishment of Society for the Improvement of Naval Architecture	Massacre of Champs de Mars in Paris. Thomas Paine publishes *Rights of Man*.
1792	Living in Red Lion Square, with workshop		Start of the French Revolutionary Wars (1792–1802)
1793			William Godwin publishes *Political Justice*. Louis XVI is executed in Paris.

Year	Nicholson's home and family	Nicholson's employment, inventions, patents	Nicholson's world
1794			Holcroft arrested in treason trials. French chemist and tax collector Antoine Lavoisier is executed.
1795	Living in Great Russell Street. Catherine Nicholson born.	Builds gravity escapement clock. Launch of Nicholson's *Journal*.	Josiah Wedgwood dies. Bread riots across the country.
1796	Living in Newman Street (with mechanical shop over stables at the bottom of the yard)	Witness in patent dispute *Boulton & Watt v Hornblower & Maberly*	Construction starts for world's first prisoner of war camp for 4000 prisoners from West Indies at Norman Cross
1797	Charlotte Nicholson born (16 April)		Mary Wollstonecraft dies giving birth to Mary Shelley (née Godwin)
1798			Edward Jenner publishes results of his vaccination experiment
1799	Moves to 10 Soho Square. Martha May Nicholson born.	Establishes school at 10 Soho Square. Advertises series of philosophical lectures and conversations.	Royal Institution of Great Britain founded. Battle of Seringapatam: Sultan of Mysore's kingdom is divided between East India Co. and Hyderabad.
1800		Nicholson and Anthony Carlisle decompose water by using voltaic pile, a process later called electrolysis	Alessandro Volta builds the first chemical battery. Richard Trevithick invents first high-pressure steam engine.
1801		Appointed to Chemical Committee at the Royal Institution	Humphry Davy is appointed Director of Laboratory at the Royal Institution

Year	Nicholson's home and family	Nicholson's employment, inventions, patents	Nicholson's world
1802		Patent 2641: file-making machine. Consulting to Richard Trevithick on patent.	End of the French Revolutionary Wars (1792–1802). Peel's Factory Act requires education for apprentices.
1803			Start of the Napoleonic Wars (1803–1815)
1804		Agent to Thomas Pitt, 2nd Baron Camelford	Trevithick's Penydarren steam engine runs on rails
1805			Bill calling for the abolition of slavery fails for the eleventh time. Joseph Louis Gay-Lussac discovers that water is two parts of hydrogen to one oxygen.
1806	Nicholson in Fleet prison over £12,000 in debt	Appointed to West Middlesex Waterworks. Patent 2990: improvements in the application of steam	Napoleon declares the Continental Blockade against the British; blocks British exports to Europe
1807	Debt problems, and visit(s) to King's Bench	Dismissed from West Middlesex Waterworks. Consultant to Koenig while in King's Bench.	Abolition of Slave Trade Act is passed. Geological Society of London is founded.
1808	Death of daughter Mary in India	Goes to Portsmouth to survey for waterworks	Humphry Davy constructs giant voltaic pile. John Dalton publishes his atomic theory.
1809		Act of Parliament passed for Portsea Island Water Works	The Theatre Royal, Drury Lane, is destroyed in a fire
1810			William Wordsworth publishes Guide to the Lakes

Year	Nicholson's home and family	Nicholson's employment, inventions, patents	Nicholson's world
1811		First water piped to homes in Portsmouth	Friedrich Koenig produces the first steam printing press
1812		Elected to Geological Society. Patent 3514: suspension of wheel carriages.	Ninety-six miners die in the Felling Mine disaster
1813	Living in Bloomsbury Square. Faces bankruptcy proceedings.	Nicholson's *Journal* merges with Alexander Tilloch's *Philosophical Journal*	Charter Act ends monopoly of East India Company, except with China and the tea trade
1814	Living in Charlotte Street		*The Times* is printed on a cylindrical printing machine. Gas Light and Coke Company installs first street lighting.
1815	Died 21 May; buried in St George's Burial Grounds		End of Napoleonic Wars (1803–1815). Humphry Davy invents the miner's safety lamp, aided by Michael Faraday. Publication of William Smith's Geological Map. Ada Lovelace born.

Dates unknown for birth of Isaac and two other children.

THE LIFE
OF WILLIAM
NICHOLSON
by His Son

Published for the first time from the original manuscript
of 1868

'The true origin of all that has been done in electro-chemical science was the accidental discovery of Messrs Nicholson and Carlisle, of the decomposition of water by the pile of Volta, 30 April 1800. These gentlemen immediately added to this capital fact, the knowledge of the decomposition of certain metallic solutions, and the circumstance of the separation of alkali on the negative plates of the apparatus.

Mr Cruikshank, in pursuing their experiments, added to them many important new results, such as the decomposition of muriates of magnesia, soda and ammonia, by the pile; and that alkaline matter always appeared at the negative, and acid at the positive pole; and Dr Henry about the same time ... confirmed the general conclusions of Messrs Nicholson and Carlisle.'

— Humphry Davy, 'The Bakerian Lecture: On the Relations of Electrical and Chemical Change', *Philosophical Transactions*, Vol. 116, London, 1826, pp. 383–422

William Nicholson (1753–1815)

Engraving by Thomas Blood for the European Magazine, *1812,*
after an original painting by Samuel Drummond

Preface

I, WILLIAM NICHOLSON, now in my eightieth year, whose father William Nicholson died fifty-three years ago, have seen and heard a great deal of what passed in my father's lifetime among the most distinguished philosophers of those days.

Being now out of business and a comparatively idle man, I think good to record what I do know and like Marco Polo 'put down the things that I have seen only', and whether I am roasted or let alone by those awful reviewers I shall even offer a copy to a bookseller, who if he likes to risk his money I will risk the roasting.

For though I feel and well know that I have no pretensions to rank with the great in the world of science, yet 'In nature's infinite book of science a little I can read'!

William Nicholson
Manchester
(c.1868)

'*William Nicholson was born December 13, 1753 at 9 o'clock in the morning in Great Carter Lane, London, and was baptised by the clergyman of the parish of St Bartholomew the Less (near Smithfields). Catherine Bouillie, his wife, was born March 24, 1761 in Warwick Street, Golden Square, London, and baptised by the clergyman of St James's Church. Married at the parish church of St Giles, near the west end of Holborn, London.*'

The above is an exact copy of a memorandum written by my father in the fly-leaf of a small old prayer book.

M Y FATHER'S FATHER WAS A SOLICITOR, or in some way connected with the law, and I believe at one time a police magistrate.

Thomas Holcroft, the dramatist and actor (who was an early friend of my father),[12] says my grandfather had chambers in the Temple, but on this subject my father was always remarkably silent. He had three brothers and all took the name of their mother, implying that my father's mother was not married. Be this as it may, my father's fame rests solely on his own achievements without any ancestral claims.

At nine years of age he was sent, along with his brothers, to a cheap school near Richmond in Yorkshire; and my father, being one of the kindest and best-tempered men living, used to amuse the children with stories of this 'Do-the-boys school'.[13]

The first step in their education was to send them to harrow and plough and other farm work; and I remember his description of the hind or over-looker who came occasionally on a pony to see how the lads got on. The man appears to have been a good-natured fellow, and his appearance and broad Yorkshire dialect created great fun for the Cockney lads. He called his pony Potatoes and occasionally took one of the boys up behind him at the dinner hour. It being my father's turn to ride, he asked the man why he called the pony Potatoes and was informed that the pony had named himself, and that if he listened to the pony's feet when he set him on to canter he would hear them say potato-potato-potato, which chimes in with the footfall of the pony's canter. This and such poor jokes amused the boys and showed the good nature of this rustic wag.

---

12. Thomas Holcroft (1745–1809), liberal author and dramatist, was one of thirty men who were arrested for treason in 1794. Following the acquittals of others who had been similarly charged, the charges against Holcroft were dropped.

13. This comes from Dotheboys Hall in *The Life and Adventures of Nicholas Nickleby*, Charles Dickens, London: Chapman and Hall, 1838–9.

Next there was a small epitome of 'town and gown';[14] that is, the town boys met periodically to fight the school boys. The battlefield was near a brook or river where there was an abundant supply of ammunition in the form of stones on the riverbank; these formed the artillery, but they generally came to the charge very soon, and then sticks and fisticuffs decided the victory on one side or the other.

Then there was the fun and frolic on winter's nights when they came home to the kitchen which served for boys and all. One of their practical jokes was on the shepherd who generally fell fast asleep with his hat on, to which the boys carefully hung shreds of paper and when all was ready set a light to them, so that the poor shepherd jumped up in a blaze of fire.

However, with all this there were books at the school and the master must have done something towards educating the boys. But with my father books were enough; he mainly educated himself and very soon was so far advanced beyond his companions that the master made him a sort of monitor or usher over the whole troupe. So ready was he that at eleven years of age he translated parts of Virgil into English verse, and at fourteen he was tolerably far advanced in Latin, Greek and French – the latter of which he translated fluently but never spoke without an accent.

As time went on at this rough school he continued with limited means to make for himself a microscope and a camera obscura. The lenses were made by breaking small phials and carefully grinding the semi-spherical lump of glass at the bottom, which had afterwards to be polished on a razor strop to make a semi-convex lens. Siphons, pumps and instruments to determine the time and take altitudes were among his productions.

---

14. An expression arising from the regular disputes that arose between the townsmen and scholars in university cities such as Oxford and Cambridge.

I have a small and dirty little memorandum book[15] of my father's bearing the date 16 May 1767. At one end of the book is a cash account, very neatly kept; the entries consist of pence, threepence and sometimes a sixpence – but mostly single pence – which seems to have been his weekly allowance. The other end of the book begins with various extracts from the scriptures and a very beautiful prayer. Then a list of books, among which are Young's *Bright Thoughts*[16], Newton, Spencer, Chaucer, etc. and then some receipts. 'How to Make an Artificial Inflammable Air as in Coal Pits', and 'The Properties of Water, Oil of Vitriol and Iron Filings, Etc'. I name this to show the drift of a boy's mind at fourteen years of age.

He left the Yorkshire school when he was between fifteen and sixteen years of age and entered the service of the East India Company as midshipman on board *The Boston*,[17] and in this vessel, and afterwards in *The Gatton*,[18] he made two voyages to China.

His log book[19] is kept with his usual neatness and contains numerous sketches of the coast in the various quarters of the world he visited.[20] Returning home, after the second voyage in the year 1773, being then in his twentieth year, he determined to leave the sea and seek some occupation on shore; being most likely influenced by the death of his father which had recently taken place.

He first got employment in an attorney's office, to which he might have been introduced by his father's connections.

---

15. Whereabouts unknown.

16. This may refer to Edward Young's *The Beauties of Dr. Young's Night Thoughts*, 1769.

17. No record of an East Indiaman called *The Boston* has been found at that time.

18. *The Gatton* was launched in 1771. It had three decks, a capacity of 778 tonnes and a length of almost 139 feet (42.4 metres). Owned by George Willson; the Captain was William Money.

19. Nicholson MSS, private collection.

20. *The Gatton* sailed to Macao and Canton (now Guangzhou).

About the year 1775, he became acquainted with the celebrated Mr Josiah Wedgwood[21] and undertook an agency for the sale of pottery in Holland, where he resided some years in Amsterdam occupied in Mr Wedgwood's affairs.

I am not aware of the exact date of his return to London, but soon after his return he made the acquaintance of Holcroft, the actor and subsequent author of *The Road to Ruin*.

I rather think my father made Holcroft's acquaintance at a cheap dining house or cook shop in what was then called Porridge Island, a narrow passage or court at the back of St Martin's Church.[22] I have often heard my father talk about Porridge Island, and I remember he and Holcroft laughing together about some joke or adventure at the Island and appealing to Mr Hewlett[23] who was present. But the Reverend John Hewlett, who then kept a thriving school at Shackleford, frowned and remembered nothing about it, implying that all such vulgarity should be left dead and buried at Porridge Island.

Mr Hewlett, who afterwards became the lecturer at the Foundling Hospital, was a man of the same standing with Holcroft and my father and daily dined with them at the Island, which he now wished sunk and forgot, but nevertheless a very kind and friendly man. I remember him well.

Holcroft, in his memoirs,[24] speaks of the famed Porridge Island, and I have heard my father say a great deal to the same effect. It seems that Porridge Island was in those days a settlement of cook shops long since pulled down. The shop my father and

21. Josiah Wedgwood (1730–95), 'The Father of English Potters', who pioneered the perfection of ceramic manufacturing via experimentation from his factory in Etruria, Staffordshire. With a strong export market, Wedgwood had an agency in Amsterdam from 1773.

22. St Martin-in-the-Fields near Trafalgar Square and Charing Cross.

23. Revd John Hewlett (1762–1844), biblical scholar; from around 1802 he was the preacher at the Foundling Hospital and from 1804 lectured on belles-lettres at the Royal Institution.

24. William Hazlitt and Thomas Holcroft, *Memoirs of the Late Thomas Holcroft*, Book I, London: Longman, Hurst, Rees, Orme and Brown, 1816, pp. 104–6.

his friends frequented consisted of the shop and kitchen on the ground floor. In the shop were tables and benches where casual customers might get a plate of the smoking meal exhibited in the window; but the select company went upstairs, and up those stairs walked my father, Holcroft, Godwin,[25] Hewlett, Shield (the composer of *Love in a Village*)[26] and other men well known to the world. The room in which they went for a ninepenny[27] dinner ran the whole length of the house and was furnished with a long table and high-backed wooden chairs.

They had one constant chairman or president, an old Irish gentleman, who informed you the first thing that his father was a bishop and expected great deference from everyone in consequence. He was submitted to partly in earnest and partly in joke. On his arrival, he first put away his umbrella, then took off his great coat and fastened it with a long pin to the back of one of the high-backed chairs. He then formally paid his respects to the company and the chair in form. He was a man of letters, had travelled much and was endless in his quotations, especially from Milton. His name was Cannon, and the company called themselves Cannonians in honour of the great man.

Holcroft had a never-ending fund of anecdotes and was a man of great energy, having been a half-starved donkey driver as a boy, a Newmarket jockey, a strolling player with Kemble's Company,[28] where Shield played the first fiddle to three or four

---

25. William Godwin (1756–1836) was an author and political philosopher who believed in the 'perfectibility' of man via education and enlightenment, publishing his ideas in *An Enquiry Concerning Political Justice* in 1793. Godwin maintained a diary from 1788 and records more thanr five hundred meetings with Nicholson. In 1797 Godwin married the feminist journalist and author Mary Wollstonecraft, who died later that year after giving birth to their daughter who was to become Mary Shelley.

26. William Shield (1748/9–1829), composer and violinist, Master of the King's Musick from 1817 to 1820.

27. Approximately £4.60 in 2017. RPI equivalent via *www.measuringworth.com*, accessed 12 November 2017.

28. Established by Roger Kemble (1722–1802), actor and theatre manager.

others, and was by then a song writer to Ann Catley at Vauxhall.[29] All these matters he used to talk about freely and amuse us boys with his horde lore.

Godwin was more quiet but very sententious and what he said was always to the purpose.

Hewlett, a happy cheerful man, would always have his joke but always appeared to me to soon get weary of scientific conversation.

Shield, the composer, would chiefly shine in theatrical anecdote and former adventures with his friend Holcroft.

My father and the great Cannon in the chair would assimilate the best; but still he had a ready appreciation of the ludicrous, and his amiable, placid and kind temperament always made him a great favourite in all company. From my knowledge of the men, I suspect this ninepenny dinner displayed an amount of wit and intellect not always met with at the first tables of the nobles of the land.

Holcroft's song writing for Vauxhall seems to have put him a little ahead of his companions, for at this time he took and furnished one of the large old-fashioned houses on the east side of Southampton Row. Here he proposed that my father should lodge with him, which he did, and Holcroft wrote one of his earliest plays called *Duplicity: A Comedy, in Five Acts*.[30] My father wrote the prologue, and play and prologue were both damned on the second or third night of the performance. I have no doubt that it was by the persuasion of Holcroft that my father was induced to try his hand at this branch of literature for which he was by no means qualified.

Nevertheless, he continued to write essays, poems and light literature for the periodicals of the day, to none of which he put his name, nor did I ever hear him allude to them in later life.

---

29. Ann Catley (1745–89), actress and soprano; later known as Mrs Lascelles. Vauxhall Gardens on the south bank of the Thames was the most significant of the Georgian pleasure gardens.

30. First performed at the Theatre Royal, Covent Garden, in October 1781.

A T THE SAME TIME HE WAS THUS PARTLY OCCUPIED WITH
HOLCROFT, his mind was mainly engaged and his time
devoted to his first scientific work, *An Introduction to
Natural Philosophy*, which he published in 1782.

This was a far more congenial feat for his genius than prologues
and poems, and at once stamped him as an authority in the world
of science. The work was published in two octavo volumes by
Messrs Johnson[31] of St Paul's Church Yard and was immediately
introduced into the universities and other schools of education so
that my father's position and prospects assumed quite a new and
more fitting character.

My father's connection with Messrs Johnson (the leading
booksellers) in his first successful work would necessarily lead him
to listen to any suggestion of theirs as to future operations; and at
their suggestion he undertook the translation of Voltaire's recent
work on the philosophy of Newton.[32]

Of this work, Voltaire says in his memoir:

*I was the first who dared unfold to my countrymen in an intelligible
style the discoveries of the great Newton. The Cartesian prejudices
which had taken the place of the prejudices of the peripatetics were
at the time so rooted in the minds of the French that the Chancellor
d'Aquesseau regarded any man whatever who should adopt
discoveries made in England as an enemy to reason and the State.
He never would grant a privilege that I might have my* Elements
of the Newtonian Philosophy *printed.*[33]

---

31. Joseph Johnson (1738–1809), 'Father of the Book Trade', a liberal publisher of works on
the arts, science, politics and religion. Considered an English Jacobin, he employed Mary
Wollstonecraft and published Joseph Priestley, Erasmus Darwin, Thomas Paine, Humphry
Davy and Thomas Beddoes.

32. No record has been found to indicate that Joseph Johnson published a translation of Voltaire's
Elémens de la Philosophie de Neuton of 1738 or that a translation of this by Nicholson was
published elsewhere.

33. Quoting from Voltaire, *Memoirs of the Life of Voltaire*, written by Voltaire and translated from the
French [by Thomas Holcroft], printed for G. Robinson, 25 Paternoster Row, London, 1784, p. 60.

Printed, however, they were, and the priesthood denied Voltaire a Christian burial in pure spite for this and other services which that great man performed for mankind.

This epitome of the great Newton my father translated into English as his second appearance before the public in his true character of a philosopher, and henceforth he had no more to do with prologues or poems for which he was quite unfitted, the bias of his mind being essentially mathematical and inductive.

The success of *The Introduction to Natural Philosophy* and other works of this period enabled my father to marry, at twenty-eight years of age, and he left Holcroft's house for lodgings which he took for my mother in Warwick Street, Golden Square.

In a memorandum of the birth of his first child he says, it was 'at the fourth house to the north of Leicester Street including the corner house and on the west side of the street that is Warwick Street'. I copy this only to show his habitual neatness and precision in everything, however unimportant it might be, and I find this sort of minute memorandum of the birth of every child. He had twelve children in all.

For myself, he says: 'William Nicholson born at 27 New North Street, Red Lion Square, being the house immediately to the north of Bedford Court on the west side of the street. Saturday 31 October 1789.'

From Warwick Street he had moved to various lodgings in London, but the house in New North Street was the first home he furnished on his own account.

From New North Street he removed to the house in the north-east corner of Red Lion Square in which I have the earliest recollection of seeing my godfather Mr Magellan;[34] and at this

---

34. Jean Hyacinthe de Magellan (1722–90), born in Portugal. After travelling extensively in Europe and developing an important network of scientific correspondents, he arrived in London in 1763 and established himself as an agent for scientific instruments. He was a founder member of the philosophical society established by Richard Kirwan in 1780, to which he proposed Nicholson for membership in 1783.

period his mechanical inventions must have been in progress, as George Deyerlein, the mechanic,[35] was occasionally in consultation with my father.

From Red Lion Square my father removed to Great Russell Street and next to Newman Street which was at the time a colony of artists and scientific characters. There resided Holcroft, John Bacon the sculptor,[36] Thomas Stothard the artist[37] and many other men of talent. Here in Newman Street my father was still pursuing his mechanical inventions, and there was a mechanical shop fitted up over the stables at the bottom of the yard.

Good George Deyerlein and another mechanic worked at the bench and lathe, and the lumber of the place and the work going on round it was an Eldorado for myself and my brother to rummage and play in.

The war and the French Revolution were great subjects of the day, and the mechanic was constantly telling George Deyerlein the sayings and doings of the political society to which he belonged. They thought we boys were too young to take any notice, but we did.

George Deyerlein, a sober German, dissuaded the other from meddling with politics, but we thought him a hero. From what we heard in the shop and learned from Holcroft, John Thelwall[38] and others in the house we were as well posted up in the war and revolutionary affairs as most boys of our age.

My brother and I went to a school of some 150 boys (a Mr Dean's) near at hand, and the battles between French and English[39] were a constant game in play hours.

---

35. John George Deyerlein (1767–1826), engineer.
36. John Bacon (1740–99), a figurative sculptor whose works include the statue of William III in St James Square, lived at 17 Newman Street.
37. Thomas Stothard (1755–1834), a prolific illustrator and painter, lived at 28 Newman Street.
38. John Thelwall (1764–1834), political reformer and educationist, was arrested and tried for treason in 1794 but was acquitted.
39. The wars of the French Revolution (1792–1802).

I remember we had an occasional man servant who came to do odd jobs about the house. He was called 'Old Clements'. He also worked at Holcroft's and some others, but his mainstay was Mr Bacon the sculptor, and to Mr Bacon's studio I was introduced by Old Clements. When we went in Mr Bacon, who was in his dishabille modelling the statue of William III which now stands in St James's Square, received me very kindly when he heard that I was the son of Mr Nicholson and showed me how he managed the clay. Clements was engaged mixing the plaster which was about to be used and seemed to me, as a boy, to have obtained the entire confidence of his master. Mr Bacon kindly explained everything to me, and I saw them successfully take a plaster mould of the clay head of the figure.

Clements was a garrulous, splay-footed, good-natured fellow. He had been a smuggler in his youth and used to make me and my brother stare at the recital of his adventures: how there was always a cask of rum on deck for them to help themselves, and that this being restricted they threatened to throw the leader overboard and then get more rum than ever; how the revenue cutters pursued them but never could catch them; and how they landed cargo at midnight and put on smock frocks to cart the kegs up country. Clements was an invaluable man: carpenter, smith and jack of all trades.

A T THIS TIME, MY FATHER'S HOUSE IN NEWMAN STREET was the constant resort of Holcroft, Godwin, Thelwall and others who deeply interested themselves in the politics of the day. On these occasions my father's habitual good nature made him listen and make an occasional remark, but he by no means joined in the political opinions which were sometimes advocated. On one occasion when Holcroft and Thelwall called and pressed him to acquiesce in some opinions they thought of importance, he distinctly told them how far he differed from their way of thinking: after which I think their meetings were less frequent.

Godwin, who had a very severe deportment, a penthouse[40] brow and deliberate speech, was rather a terror to the children, though he generally noticed us and was rather good-natured than otherwise. But he had an abominable trick of asking us to spell. For instance, he would catch me and, holding me between his knees, begin, 'Now, suppose you had four apples, how do you spell four?' Then, 'The foreleg of a horse. How do you spell that?' Of course we were sometimes right and sometimes wrong, but we were unanimous in thinking we had enough of this sort of thing at school without being bored with an amateur performance at home.

Holcroft was an uncertain customer, sometimes in a good temper and sometimes not, but having had the misfortune to burn the skin off his face in an attempt to harden his feet with vitriolic acid and water he did not look all that prepossessing to our young eyes.

Nevertheless the tales of his former life which he occasionally narrated in conversation with my father always interested us and made him an important personage: how he had slept in the straw along with a horse under his care in the stables at Newmarket

---

40. Prominent.

when a boy and how careful the horse was not to tread upon him when he got up. To which my father, doubting the horse's good manners, said it arose from the same sort of feeling which would have prevented him treading on a garden roller if laid beside him. Holcroft also told us how on his tramp on foot with a strolling company of players the best thing was worsted stockings to keep the skin on your feet, and how he and Shield had walked from Durham to Stockton-on-Tees in quick time with little or nothing to eat on the road.

But he was very satirical and, though he and I as a boy were good friends enough, he often hurt my feelings by quizzing me and my walking stick which was a present from a friend and of which I had the highest opinion.

Thelwall was far more courteous than either, a neatly dressed little gentleman who invited me to the first evening party I ever went to. He was at that time living in a street turning out from Bedford Square and undertook to teach elocution and cure impediments in the speech.

I remember on my entering the room the company were seated in a circle, with Thelwall standing and speaking to them. He welcomed me with great politeness and I took a chair near the door, but seeing Fanny Holcroft,[41] whom I knew, on the opposite side of the room I walked across and entered into conversation with her.

Thelwall immediately came up to us and made a speech which rather put me to the blush. He commenced by saying, 'The age of Chivalry should never die while he and I survive!' The fact was that the young gentlemen of the party were most of his pupils with impediments in their speech, and being strangers to the ladies they were rather diffident in commencing conversation.

41. Fanny Holcroft (1780–1844), daughter of Thomas Holcroft, was an author and poet known primarily for her abolitionist poem 'The Negro', 1797.

However, as the shyness wore off we got on very well, and I am afraid Fanny and I, who were old friends, behaved the worst of any. The various styles of stuttering and other impediments which were presented to our observation during the evening set Fanny and I on the titter; and those who remember how little will set boys and girls laughing when they ought to behave themselves may imagine what difficulty we had to restrain ourselves from bursting out. Thelwall was hospitable, but nevertheless he maintained a sort of theatrical dignity throughout.

He told us, among other things, that while standing on a hill near Bristol he saw a man-of-war ship at sea in the distance, that as he was looking on she fired a salute, and almost instantaneously after seeing the flash he heard the sound, from which he inferred that sound passed upwards quicker than in another direction; which at the time I thought was a mistake.

From some experiments communicated lately to the Paris Academy of Sciences by Monsieur Flammarion[42] it appears Mr Thelwall was right in his remark. Monsieur Flammarion said 'that having ascended in a balloon at 3,000 metres he heard the railway whistle, at 2,500 the noise of the train along with a gun and a dog barking, at 1,000 the noise of the crowd, cows, cocks crowing and the human voice, but he could not make himself heard down below from 100 metres!'

However, the party went off very well on the whole, and Fanny and I walked home to Newman Street and had many a laugh at the poor stuttering gentlemen afterwards.

Another remarkable and very learned person who was then our constant visitor was a Dr Gruber, a German who spoke remarkably good English. He was a well-dressed, middle-aged, short and broad-set man who stooped; I thought him rather deformed in

---

42. Nicolas Camille Flammarion (1842–1925), French astronomer and author.

his back. He lodged on the second floor in a house in Castle Street four or five doors from the market on the north side of the street. The first floor below him was occupied by Barry, an artist who painted for the Society of Arts,[43] and the ground floor by some French refugees.

Here I was frequently sent by my father with notes for the doctor, who had valuable books and various philosophical apparatus in his rooms. He had an air pump and an electrical machine and other matters which he allowed me to examine and use under his direction, to my great delight. Besides which he always had something good in the way of cakes or apples or grapes of which he was by no means a niggard.

My father often spoke of him as a very learned man and I could remember how greatly he enjoyed the doctor's conversation, which was heightened by his extreme good temper and the courtly manners of a perfect gentleman. I rather think he had some peculiar views regarding electricity, as that was the constant theme of their conversation and a subject in which my father at that time was engaged and deeply interested. He was kindness and courtesy itself, and he soon gained my mother's admiration, by his admiration of her children and pleasing conversation on any subject whatever, from anatomy to pudding compounds, when my father was away. But let Father return, electricity resumed its power, and the doctor and he were mutually attracted to each other and conversed together for the remainder of the visit.

At length, Dr Gruber formally invited my father, mother and family to tea, and we all went excepting the baby. There was an abundance of good things, and my mother made tea. Then the electrical machines were in order, also the air pump, and we saw

43. James Barry (1741–1806), the artist whose six-part series of paintings entitled *The Progress of Human Culture* hangs in the Great Room of the Royal Society of Arts, lived at 36 Castle Street.

paper figures dance and a guinea and a feather fall under the receiver in equal time and we sat down on a chair (which was a bellows) that squealed like a cat.

This feasting occurred more than once, and though the staircase was lumbered with Barry's picture frames, when you arrived at the second floor all was clean and comfortable. I think there were three rooms on the floor. The front and adjoining room were crowded with books and some old paintings, and in the centre of the mantelpiece in the back room stood a crucifix with the figure of Christ, indicating that the doctor was a Roman Catholic.

The whole affair was a great treat to every one of us, and the lavish expenditure used to make us stare. I think the first pineapple[44] I ever tasted was cut after tea at Dr Gruber's second-floor lodging in Castle Street.

This end of Castle Street consisted of poor lodgings at this time mainly occupied by French emigrants, with whom we used to think Dr Gruber in some way connected, but knew no more.

Godwin, Thelwall, Holcroft and others were constantly at our house, and, though my father never evinced any very strong political bias, the others expressed themselves very forcibly, and there was constant reference to a Corresponding Society[45] from which great things were expected to result. To all this did Dr Gruber most seriously incline his ear though he said little, until he and my father got on some scientific subject, which partly shut out the others.

---

44. Pineapples had been grown in the Netherlands since the 1680s and in Britain since around 1716, after which their growing became something of a competitive sport in Georgian society as hot-house technology developed.

45. The London Corresponding Society was an association of tradespeople between 1792 and 1799 founded to consider 'how to remedy the many defects and abuses which had crept into the administration of government'. Thomas Hardy (1752–1832), who was secretary and treasurer, was arrested and tried for treason in 1794.

The Bible and Crown, at no. 32 Cornhill, was an established bookseller's shop, kept in those days by a Mr Sewell,[46] a man of considerable literary attainments and a friend of my father. To this shop Dr Gruber used to resort daily between four and five o'clock. Being an important customer for periodicals and books, he was allowed to mount a sort of pulpit desk, which overlooked the whole shop, for the purpose of writing a letter. This he did almost daily. And daily congregated in the shop after change time in the City six or eight or more of London's leading merchants to gossip over politics and the affairs of the day, which between 1795 and 1798 were of rather an exciting character[47] and which Dr Gruber necessarily overheard.

Time passed, and we lost sight of Dr Gruber and his pleasant ways. But about twenty years ago I met with a most intelligent German gentleman who came from Vienna, and I incidentally chanced to name Dr Gruber and his doings. The gentleman told me he knew him well, that his name was not Gruber, that he was very high in the Catholic Church in Vienna and highly connected. That his vocation in London when we saw so much of him was that of a political spy: that his object at my father's house was not electricity but the progress of the Corresponding Society and the political opinions of Holcroft, Thelwall and his set. The writing in Sewell's shop was a record of the gossip of the day among city men of good standing, which was of course periodically forwarded to his government.

If it was so, which I have no reason to doubt, it was cleverly done, and he acted his part to perfection. I am more inclined to

---

46. John Sewell (1735–1802), a publisher with close links to the East India Company; one of the publishers of Nicholson's *The Navigator's Assistant* in 1784 and founder of the Society for the Improvement of Naval Architecture in 1791.

47. Riots over food shortages (the bread riots) were common in 1795 and 1796 throughout Britain. In one massive demonstration in London in October 1795 protestors hissed at King George III and demanded 'Give us peace and bread!' and 'No war, no famine, no Pitt, no king!'

think this gentleman's statement the true explanation as I once heard the doctor relate an anecdote of a spy (which might have been himself).

He said the spy had run over from Dover to the coast of France in an open boat on a calm night, that he spoke French like a native, had no luggage and was landed away from any town on the beach. Walking along, he met a fisherman who directed him to a village inn, which he entered and called for what refreshment he required, and then he sat down for a smoke among the general company. All went on as a matter of course until someone asked which way he had come. His ignorance of the locality made his situation rather awkward.

The man who sat next to him very soon identified that the spy came from England and he was marched off to the Prefect forthwith. There the truth soon liberated him, as he was a spy not for, but against, England.[48] He asked the man who had detected him, and who was one of the Police, how he had found him out. He then learned that when he leaned forward to light his pipe the man had gently turned up one of the brass buttons on the back of his coat and seen the word 'Birmingham', which explained everything.

---

48. Espionage was rife at this time, as both British and French governments sought intelligence on each other's political developments, radical activities and public protests. Industrial espionage was also a growing problem and was an issue that Wedgwood, Nicholson and Matthew Boulton addressed via the General Chamber of Manufacturers.

DOUBTLESS MY FATHER SOON DISCOVERED, after his connection with the Johnsons, how much better were his then pursuits than toiling on the sea, and he and Holcroft lived many years together in the house in Southampton Row in considerable comfort.[49]

The Johnsons soon found out what a valuable ally my father might prove from his varied information and proposed the republication of Ralph's *A Critical Review of the Public Buildings, Statues, and Ornaments, in and about London and Westminster*, to which he made great additions.[50]

In 1783 he published *The Navigator's Assistant* in one octavo volume, a work which he had put together many years before, the greater part while he was in the service of the East India Company.

There followed a translation of the *History of Hyder Shah, alias Hyder Ali Khan Bahadur, or New Memoirs Concerning the East Indies with Historical Notes*, which was praised as a spirited translation but seems to me quite as much out of my father's line as his unfortunate prologues and poems.[51]

About 1785 Mr Wedgwood, being appointed Chairman of the General Chamber of Manufacturers of Great Britain and Ireland,[52] proposed my father as secretary.

---

49. William Nicholson Junior's recollections return now to the late 1770s and early 1780s.

50. This was not published by J. Johnson but by J. Wallis, 1783.

51. Sultan Ayder Ali Khan was 'the most famous conqueror India has beheld', ruling the kingdom of Mysore in India from 1761. Nicholson's interest is less surprising when you consider that his first voyage with the East India Company coincided with the first Anglo-Mysore war (1767–9), the first of a series of wars involving the British and the French between the East India Company and the Kingdom under Ayder Ali Khan.

52. The General Chamber of Manufacturers of Great Britain and Ireland (1785–7) was an umbrella group to coordinate the interests of local chambers of commerce and to provide 'a permanent representative industrial association, to watch over their interests as one aggregate'. A key activity was protesting and lobbying, and the group's motto was 'Every petition has its weight.' Unfortunately, aside from opposition to the proposed Irish Treaty, there were few other issues of common interest and the organization folded after a few years.

In this appointment he displayed great industry, and besides the immediate business of the day he published *An Abstract of Such Acts of Parliament as Are Now in Force, for Preventing the Exportation of Wool and other Commodities, Tools, and Implements Used in the Manufactures Thereof: and Also for Preventing the Seducing of Artists into Foreign Parts*, a pamphlet showing the impolicy of restraining the export of any raw material.

During this secretaryship he evinced great knowledge of statistics, finance, political economy and in no small degree added to the fame of the association.

While my father was thus occupied, and gaining reputation in the world of science, he found time to translate the voluminous chemical works of Fourcroy, which were published between 1788 and 1804.[53]

He also communicated to the Royal Society some invention in electrical apparatus, a subject to which he had long devoted much time and attention. This was the revolving doubler for measuring minute quantities of electricity and a spinning instrument for the same purpose, both of which were highly appreciated and published in the *Philosophical Transactions* of the Royal Society of that period.

Electricity was always a favourite study of my father's, and he published in the *Philosophical Transactions* in the same way a long paper on the excitation of electricity, the nature of positive and negative states, with the results of many experiments that he was then engaged on.[54]

---

53. Antoine François, comte de Fourcroy (1755–1809), French chemist. In 1788 Nicholson published the four-volume translation of Fourcroy's *Elements of Natural History, and of Chemistry*. In 1789 he translated and annotated its *Supplement*. In 1801 he translated the *Synoptic Tables of Chemistry*, and in 1804 he published *A General System of Chemical Knowledge* in eleven volumes.

54. Three papers by Nicholson were read to the Royal Society on the subjects of logarithms (1787), the revolving doubler (1788) and electricity (1789). It is possible that Nicholson is also 'Mr Nicholson', who wrote a paper on the subject of lightning, communicated to the Royal Society by Joseph Priestley in 1774.

At this time there was a controversy going on between his friend Mr Richard Kirwan the chemist[55] and the French Academy on phlogiston.[56] On this controversy my father published an elaborate criticism on the amount of confidence to which some experiments on the decomposition of water were entitled.[57]

---

55. Richard Kirwan (1733–1812), chemist and geologist who founded the philosophical society that first met at the Chapter Coffee House in 1780.

56. As natural philosophers sought to understand heat and inflammability, one theory was based upon a supposed element called phlogiston. The theory of phlogiston was strongly supported by Richard Kirwan and Joseph Priestley and described by Nicholson in 1782 as 'that by which bodies, when in contact with pure air, and heated to a certain degree, are put into a state of combustion, during which they are in great measure decompounded, and most commonly, or perhaps universally, exhibit an appearance of flame'.

57. The French chemists, led by Antoine-Laurent Lavoisier (1743–94), doubted the phlogiston theory and put forward an alternative explanation based upon a new chemical nomenclature. In 1787 Richard Kirwan published a critique of Lavoisier's approach in *An Essay on Phlogiston and the Constitution of Acids*. This was translated into French by Marie-Anne Pierette Paulze (Lavoisier's wife) and published with critical notes added by French chemists de Morveau, Lavoisier, de la Place, Monge, Berthollet and Fourcroy. Nicholson translated the annotated French version into English in 1789.

To RETURN A FEW YEARS BACK, my father had not only undertaken the various vocations just spoken of but also became a member and took the secretaryship of what was called the Chapter Coffee House Society, a meeting which comprised most of the men of note in the scientific world in England.

I have the minute book of their meetings from 1780 to 1787, written by my father[58], and a most interesting document it is. It is written with his usual neatness and embellished with minute pen sketches of various experimental apparatus used by the society for pursuing their investigations.

As regards this book, the list of members is by no means the least interesting part [see APPENDIX C]. The list is found in the first leaves of the society's *Book A*. It has no date and appears to have been written in parts at various times and by various persons, though some part of it must have been extracted from the book of minutes; yet it is the only written record with respect to the original members.[59] The meetings were held every alternate week.

Many of the gentlemen continued to visit at our house, and I remember some of them well. Mr Kirwan was an Irish gentleman well known as a chemist. He wrote and published about this period *The Elements of Minerology* and some geological essays together with *An Essay on the Analysis of Mineral Waters*.

Mr Magellan was a descendant of the celebrated Ferdinand Magellan (or Magelhaens), the Portuguese navigator who discovered the strait bearing his name in the year 1519. He was, as I have said, my godfather and often noticed me kindly when he called at our house. More substantially, he showed good feeling by

---

58. The original minute book is held by the Museum of the History of Science, University of Oxford: *Minutes of the Coffee House Philosophical Society, 1780–87*, MS Gunther 4. A detailed analysis of the full membership and the minutes has been published by Trevor H. Levere and Gerard L'E. Turner in *Discussing Chemistry and Steam: The Minutes of a Coffee House Philosophical Society 1780–1787*, Oxford: Oxford University Press, 2002.

59. Nicholson's minute book is not a complete record of the society's membership.

leaving me one hundred pounds[60] placed in the hands of the Lord Chancellor; this I received when I came of age, with accrued interest.

I remember he was a tall, serious-looking man dressed in plain brown like a Quaker, but very good-natured and placid. It was he who proposed my father as a member of the Society, and in looking through the minutes I find him a frequent speaker. Of all the members he seems to have had the largest foreign correspondence, from which he often read extracts; thus:

1783 Mr Magellan read an extract from Italy in which his correspondent informs him that Count Saluces[61] has discovered a method of converting the vitriolic and marine acids into the nitrons: that Moscati has succeeded in his attempt to make platina, and that de Morveau[62] had found a menstrum that dissolved diamonds.

Mr Magellan read likewise a letter from Bergman[63] in which he candidly acknowledged that the opinion he formerly entertained respecting the production of silicous earth by fluoric acids was not well founded.

Then came a letter from Mr Cigna[64] containing an account of the absorption of air by ignited charcoal accompanied by a table comprising the results of experiments made by Count de Morozzo[65] on the above substance, then follows the table, and finally a letter from Dr Janssen, a physician in Holland, giving a circumstantial account of the good effects of injecting fixed air in cases of putrid fever.

60. Magellan died in 1790. In 2016, £100 would be equivalent to approximately £11,000 using RPI or £137,000 using average earnings. *www.measuringworth.com*, accessed 12 November 2017.

61. Giuseppe Angelo Saluzzo di Menusiglio (1734–1810), Comte de Saluces, one of the founders of the Turin Academy of Sciences.

62. Louis-Bernard Guyton, Baron de Morveau (1737–1816), French chemist and politician.

63. Torbern Olaf Bergman (1735–84), Swedish chemist.

64. Giovanni Francesco Cigna (1734–90), Italian physician.

65. Carlo Lodovico Morozzo of Bianzè (1744–1804), mathematician and physicist, president of the Academy of Sciences of Turin.

This shows Mr Magellan to have an extensive correspondence with the learned men of his day. I need not enlarge more on this interesting book of minutes as I shall hereafter add an abstract of the whole.[66]

The Society for the Improvement of Naval Architecture was established in 1791. It owed its origin to Mr John Sewell, my father's old friend, at whose request my father became a member from the first and devoted his time and talent to its advancement with his usual energy.

Among the distinguished names comprised in their meetings were to be found Sir John Borlase Warren,[67] Sir Joseph Banks,[68] Admiral Knowles,[69] Professor Martyn,[70] Colonel Beaufoy,[71] Captain William Lockyer[72] and a long list of the most prominent men of the day in science and naval knowledge. [See APPENDIX D for details of the committee of the Society for the Improvement of Naval Architecture in 1791.]

Colonel Beaufoy was a constant visitor at our house, and in after days I used to go frequently with his son to a Sunday dinner at his house at Hackney. Beaufoy was a fine handsome-looking soldier and at the time I saw him a widower. His house was then quite in the country with a beautiful garden, where young Beaufoy and I used to make free with the fruit before our Sunday dinner.

---

66. This is not included here, and we direct readers to *Discussing Chemistry and Steam*. See footnote 58.

67. Sir John Borlase Warren, baronet (1753–1822), naval officer and Member of Parliament.

68. Sir Joseph Banks, baronet (1743–1820), naturalist and long-serving president of the Royal Society (1778–1820).

69. Sir Charles Henry Knowles, second baronet (1754–1813) and naval officer.

70. Revd Thomas Martyn (1735–1825), Professor of Botany at Cambridge University and secretary to the Society for the Improvement of Naval Architecture.

71. Colonel Mark Beaufoy (1764–1827), astronomer and physicist who demonstrated the friction component of a ship's resistance.

72. William Lockyer captained young Horatio Nelson as a second lieutenant on the frigate *Lowestoffe* in 1777.

WITH HIS LITERARY LABOURS ON HAND, along with the time and attention required for the positions he held in various societies in which he was either secretary or an active member, an ordinary man might have found full occupation. But not so with my father. During this time he had always two or three mechanics employed on various machines of his own designing or invention.

I remember one of the mechanics well, George Deyerlein, a German, a burly, powerful man who used to be very good-natured to us children. He afterwards established a shop in conjunction with another German at Charing Cross under the title of Holtzapffel and Deyerlein.[73] Good George, I remember him to this day with affection.

There was a machine for cutting combs, another for cutting files and another for cylinder printing [see APPENDIX B]. Anyone who knows the toil of doing and undoing in any new mechanical arrangement will know the time and trouble it requires to perfect a new piece of machinery.

Three years or more of my father's life were spent on these three machines, for the tools and appliances were very different in those days. I think I see dear George Deyerlein rubbing away at a piece of metal with a four-square file weighing half a stone for what seemed hours, which would now be ripped down in five minutes under the planing machine and infinitely better done. However, with such means as they had then they cobbled together my father's inventions.

These mechanical speculations proved a sad loss to my father who seems little to have known the expense, trouble and difficulty of introducing any new manipulation or machinery to an established manufacture.

The opposition to any innovation in an established manufacture was well expressed to me by one of the leading manufacturers

---

73. John Jacob Holtzapffel set up his business in 1794, manufacturing lathes and tools, and took Johann Georg Deyerlein into partnership in 1804.

in Lancashire. On making some observation on possible improvement in his machinery, he said, 'To be plain with you, I wish all inventors hanged. We are doing very well and don't want to be disturbed by any alterations.' On a subsequent occasion Mr Thomas Houldsworth, one of the most important cotton spinners of the day,[74] when talking on some improvements his nephew had proposed, boasted to me that he had made his money by the bad machinery and hated the improvements.

This sort of feeling, which I witnessed ten years ago in Lancashire [c.1858], was in my father's day ten times stronger. Nevertheless, though his inventions were a great loss to him, they ultimately became, every one of them, a great gain to the public.

The comb-making machine, slightly varied from my father's model, is in general use. The file-making machine[75] is in extensive operation under the management of a joint stock company in Manchester. The cylinder printing[76] has nearly superseded the block in calico printing, and in letter-press printing on paper it is very generally used where the amount of work to be done is of sufficient magnitude or importance; for instance, *The Times* newspaper, *The Telegraph* and many provincial papers.

Mr Edward Cowper,[77] who patented some improvements in cylinder letter-press printing and constructed some of the best cylinder printing presses, used to lecture on the subject and invariably he named my father as the first inventor and the first to introduce this important improvement.

I don't mean to say the exact machines my father constructed are now in use, but every one of the present machines involve the principles on which my father's inventions were founded.

---

74. Thomas Houldsworth (1771–1852), cotton manufacturer and Member of Parliament.

75. GB 2641 of 1802.

76. GB 1748 of 1790.

77. Edward Shickle Cowper (1790–1852) delivered a lecture on improvements in printing at the Royal Institution on 22 February 1828.

A translation by my father of Chaptal's *Elements of Chemistry* from the French appeared in 1791, in three volumes, as also in 1799 a translation of *The Art of Bleaching Piece-goods, Cottons, and Threads, of Every Description, Rendered More Easy and General by Means of the Oxygenated Muriatic Acid; and with the Method of Rendering Painted or Printed Goods Perfectly White or Colourless. To Which Are Added, the Most Certain Methods of Bleaching Silk and Wool; and the Discoveries Made by the Author in the Art of Bleaching Paper* by Pajot des Charmes.[78]

He had also been occupied on *A Dictionary of Chemistry*, which appeared in 1795 in two quarto volumes. The chemical dictionary was a great success and in 1808 was condensed into a single octavo volume for more convenient reference.

This work after my father's death was pounced on by Dr Ure,[79] who first published a revised edition entitled *A Dictionary of Chemistry: On the Basis of Mr Nicholson's*, which in 1821, given the advanced state of chemical science and requirements of the times, seemed fair enough. But shortly afterwards, in a second or third edition, he coolly states in the preface in a patronizing tone that Mr Nicholson had some industry and was a candid man, etc., but as much of the matter is necessarily new there seems no good reason for retaining Mr Nicholson's name on the title page.

At the same time, a great part of the matter and the whole of the arrangement is necessarily old and verbatim as my father left it. This transaction of Dr Ure's looks very like a piece of petty larceny in literature. The broad fact as regards my father is that Dr Ure hung his name on my father's and then naïvely affected to despise the fabric which supports him. Dr Ure or any competent chemist may write a chemical dictionary, but he has no right to

---

78. Claude Pajot des Charmes (dates of birth and death unknown), French chemist and director of manufacturing company St Gobain (1805–7).

79. Andrew Ure (1778–1857), chemist.

take another man's labour and ability and adopt it as his own, dropping the name without laying himself open to the charge of fraud of which I deliberately accuse Dr Ure. Leaving Dr Ure and his shabby conduct to their fate, we proceed.

———◆———

I N 1797 MY FATHER COMMENCED NICHOLSON'S *Journal of Natural Philosophy, Chemistry and the Arts*, which was the first monthly periodical work ever published devoted exclusively to scientific subjects and inquiry in England.

This work soon obtained an extensive circulation and was read and quoted throughout Europe by all men of science and learning and is as such a record of industry and achievement in the various departments of science as few men leave behind them. The journal was originally published in quarto, of which there are five volumes, and between thirty and forty of the octavo size.

Some years before this time, my father's fame had placed him in a position to be consulted by men of science as well as engineers and manufacturers of every description.

It is ridiculous to see in his commonplace book[80] that, while he was being consulted by Richard Trevithick and Jabez Hornblower on their supposed improvements to the great Watt steam engine,[81] he had a client consulting him on the form of a quack advertisement for Gowland's Lotion![82]

Another queer affair that occurred about this time was the discovery of transparent soap. There were two brothers, Irishmen, who had a smattering of chemical knowledge, and the two schemers had managed to scheme themselves into the King's Bench Prison[83], where I called on them many a time with

---

80. Whereabouts unknown.

81. Nicholson acted as a witness for Jabez Carter Hornblower (1744–1814) and John Maberly (1770–1839) in a patent infringement case brought by Matthew Boulton and James Watt with regard to their steam engine. He appeared alongside Davies Giddy (1767–1839), who later introduced the engineer Richard Trevithick (1771–1833) to Nicholson when Trevithick sought a patent regarding his steam engine.

82. Gowland's Lotion was a facial peel preparation, comprising bitter almonds, sugar and sulphuric acid, that removed the top layer of skin.

83. Described by Nicholson in *A Critical Review* of 1783 as 'a place of confinement for debtors, and for everyone sentenced by the Court of King's Bench to suffer imprisonment; but those who can purchase the liberties have the benefit of walking through Blackman Street and a part of the borough, and to a certain distance in St George's Burial Grounds, Bloomsbury. Prisoners in any other gaol may remove hither by habeas corpus.'

notes from my father as to some grand discovery then pending. This grand discovery, whatever it was, went to the winds, and I remember the disappointment when the end arrived; but in a day or so a letter arrived urging my father to come at once and witness another real discovery.

My father took me with him for a walk, and away we went to the room of these great gentlemen in the King's Bench Prison. The room was at the very top of the first block of buildings as you entered the prison. From the window one could overlook the walls right into the country, and I remember thinking what a remarkably pleasant place it was to live in. The discovery was in a conical wine glass and came about thus: the gentlemen were in the habit of making a lather for shaving in the wine glass, which contained a small lump of soap to which hot water was added when required. When done with, the glass and soap suds were put away in a closet. In this closet there was also kept that most comfortable ingredient, Irish whiskey.

Early in the morning one gentleman, being a thirst, went to the closet and poured himself a glass of whiskey but soon discovered that he had taken the glass of soap suds, so he put it on one side and I should think took a clean glass after it. There appears to have been no more shaving for a while, for when we arrived the suds were a solid mass of semi-transparent soap; it appears that the spirit has the property of precipitating extraneous colouring matter and leaving the soap transparent – as you see it in the shops at the present day.

This lucky hit liberated the two gentlemen. My father made an arrangement with a person in the soap trade, and works were established in the Borough of Southwark which one of the gentlemen superintended.

These works I frequently visited and was always received with true Irish hospitality. They were most gentlemanly, and when the soap had washed away their difficulties I dined with them on several occasions and met some young ladies of the family from Ireland, who were certainly the handsomest women I ever saw.

The nonsense and infatuation that sometimes seems to possess inventors wants answering if it will not be profitable to witness the disappointment and heartbreaks when the bubble is burst. One poor man, who was a smith in Clerkenwell, proposed some improvement in horse shoes and had drawn and described in a rough way what he called his Orsu (horseshoe). Another Quaker gentleman suggested an idea for preventing ships foundering when they had sprung a leak by cutting a hole in the side to let the water run out.

ABOUT THIS TIME, OR A LITTLE TIME BEFORE WE LEFT
NEWMAN STREET, my father made the acquaintance of
Mr Carlisle, afterwards Sir Anthony Carlisle,[84] who I
rather think was introduced by our family doctor Dr Combe.[85]

Carlisle was at that time about thirty years of age, good-
looking and active, and what endeared him to us was his fondness
for young people. I was then myself about fourteen years old, and
he would take me with him of a morning across St James's Park to
the Westminster Hospital, where I waited until he looked around.

The exhibition of pictures at Somerset House was our great
gala day.[86] On this occasion Carlisle invited a dozen boys and
treated us all not only to the exhibition but to a good roast beef
dinner at his house in Soho Square. I remember Carlisle and I
got back from the exhibition a little before the others, and while
we were alone he pointed out to me the faint resemblance of a
cat's head in the black veins of the marble chimney place. Then
when the boys came in he told them I had discovered a great
curiosity which I would show them, giving me all the credit of his
own ingenuity. But this was the innocent sort of good nature he
indulged in.

There was at this time a gentleman studying and living in
Carlisle's house, a Mr Assay (if I spell his name right), who was
equally kind to us boys, and I was amazed at his condescension in
volunteering to go out and buy more radishes when we boys had
gobbled up all that was on the dinner table, and still more that he
helped us to make a balloon of tissue paper. In later life, Carlisle

84. Anthony Carlisle (1768–1840) was a surgeon at Westminster Hospital from 1793 and
   appointed as Professor of Anatomy to the Royal Society in 1808. He lived at 12 Soho
   Square and was involved in the decomposition of water using the voltaic pile with William
   Nicholson in 1800. He remained a lifelong friend, attending Nicholson at the end of his life.
85. Dr Charles Combe (1743–1817) focused on obstetrics. He was also a collector of medical
   equipment, coins and rare books.
86. Between 1779 and 1837 the Royal Academy was based at Somerset House, and this refers
   to its Summer Exhibition.

told me, this gentleman went to India and distinguished himself by his great attainments in the Oriental languages.

Having passed his early days at Durham and in Yorkshire, Carlisle was fond of the country and country sports. We had many a day's fishing at Carshalton, where his intimacy with the Reynolds and Shipleys procured him the use of part of the stream where the public were excluded. He was a skilful fly fisher, and during the day I generally carried the pannier and landing net, but towards night, when the mills stopped and the water ran over a bye-wash, I with my bag of worms and rod managed to hook some fish as big as were taken during the day.

We also had fishing grounds at a place in Hertford called Chennis which was rented, as I understood, by Carlisle and a fellow sportsman called Mainwaring. These two gentlemen and myself as a third in a post-chaise used to start at six o'clock, breakfast at Ware or Hoddesdon and forward to the fishing, which was fine for a boy of fourteen.

And then Mr Mainwaring always took a fowling piece with him and occasionally shot a bird which was worth all the fish, rods and lines and all.

Chennis was a remarkably quiet rural place, and the little inn we slept at was situated in a settlement of some half-dozen cottages and houses, but what its name was I do not know. On one occasion when our companion was called away Carlisle and I remained there for a day or two. We were very successful in our fishing and were about to depart when it turned out there was a county election going forward and there was no conveyance to be had for love or money. Carlisle was wanted at home, and we had no choice but to start on foot, so away we went after breakfast with a boy to show us a footpath way through fields to Rickmansworth where we hoped to get some conveyance to London.

Carlisle had the best share of the luggage and the boy and I the remainder. The country we travelled was beautifully undulated and of a dry sandy soil. It was very hot, and I suspect I was the first to feel fatigue. After a long trudge we stopped at a gate leading into a sandy lane, and looking back at the hillside I was amazed at the display of poppies in full bloom; the whole field was a mass of crimson, a new sight to me.

I was very thirsty and tired and have often thought of that field and Burns's immortal lines:

Pleasures are like poppies spread;
You seize the flower, its bloom is shed;
or like the snow fall on the river.
a moment white then melts for ever.[87]

But time, like a pitiless master, cried onward, and we had to trudge again. At last our guide left us on the dusty high road to Rickmansworth, where in time we arrived. Here we got some refreshment and awaited until a return post-chaise conveyed us to London. We had walked nearly thirty miles, and it was my first walking adventure of any magnitude.

About this time, Carlisle left his house and removed to the house at the corner of Charles Street in Soho Square. Here he was within two doors of our house, number 10, and from the terms of intimacy which existed he was frequently at our house and I as a boy was frequently at his house.

He used to allow me to accompany him to Westminster Hospital where I waited while he was engaged, and I recollect on one occasion he was consulted about the expenditure of some money for the housekeeper's room. He objected to the amount and remarked that sixpence was plenty for a looking glass and that five minutes for a man and ten minutes for a woman was

---

87. From Robert Burns, 'Tam o' Shanter', *Edinburgh Magazine*, March 1791.

plenty of time to dress in. These radical opinions highly offended the matron's dignity and produced a flood of female eloquence we could overhear where we stood. Carlisle delivered the following impromptu, whether original or not I don't know:

> 'To stop a woman's tongue, or turn the tide
> Is just as vain a job as ere was tried
> For if she will, the will you may depend on't
> and if she won't, she won't you may depend on't'.

T HE HOUSE WE HAD REMOVED TO IN SOHO SQUARE, about 1797, was number 10 and recently occupied by Messrs Arrowsmith, the map sellers. This was a very handsome house with a splendid staircase adorned with historical paintings of no mean pretensions. Here my father undertook the tuition of some ten or twelve young gentlemen, having a classical tutor and a French master to assist him. The classical tutor, from the respect shown him by the elder students, I believe to have been a learned scholar. He was a Mr Walsh, an Irishman. The other, Monsieur Gordeau, was an emigrant and the beau ideal of a Frenchman. He was a perfect gentleman, and he was respected by the young men he taught.

The Frenchman's passion for *la danse* seemed to override every other thought. He was a well-made man of thirty dressed in a sort of shabby genteel way in elastic pantaloons, very tight, and every opportunity he had of being alone in the entrance hall – and there were many – he was practising *la danse*. I was a boy of fourteen, and while the elder students were out I stole out from our study to watch Monsieur Gordeau practising *la danse* in the hall. But this was not enough for his insatiate soul. At night when we were reading or gossiping he would show us *la danse* on the table with his two forefingers in a most amazing manner. I believe he was a chevalier, and he certainly attended the soirées of the French noblesse, emigrants like himself in those days. I trust he got his own at the restoration, but *la danse* was his great passion.

During this period there were studying under my father a number of young men connected with the first families in the kingdom, and thus I do not feel warranted in mentioning all their names. Sir Richard Griffith,[88] the Kenyons,[89] Henry Ellis[90] and

88. Sir Richard John Griffith, first baronet (1784–1878), geologist, engineer and surveyor.
89. John Kenyon (1784–1856) was a poet and patron of arts. He had two brothers.
90. Sir Henry Ellis (1788–1855), diplomat, illegitimate son of Lord Hobart (see note 91).

nephews of Lord Hobart[91] have always been ready to acknowledge the debt they owed to my father for this tuition.

In 1799, my father gave a public course of lectures on natural philosophy and chemistry in Soho Square.[92] In 1804 he published a new translation of Fourcroy's *A General System of Chemical Knowledge and Its Application to the Phenomena of Nature and Art* in eleven volumes, and in 1806 he established a periodical of *General Review* in addition to his philosophical *Journal*.

The discovery of the decomposition of water by the agency of galvanism was my father's discovery and his alone. My good friend Carlisle's name has been mixed up with it by my father's good nature, which constantly allowed others to rob him of his fame.

I was present, Carlisle (who was attending one of my sisters professionally) stood by, but had no more to do with the discovery than I had, or scarcely so much, for I brought the washing basin in which it was made.[93]

The galvanic pile was constructed by Mr William Stodart,[94] the piano-forte maker whose sons at that time were at our house; it consisted of half-crowns, round pieces of zinc of the same size, and cardboards saturated with salt and water and held in a perpendicular position by wooden rods. Mr Stodart had heard or read of Volta's discovery[95] and made the pile for his own

91. Robert Hobart, 4th Earl of Buckinghamshire (1760–1816), politician.

92. Commenced 29 October 1799; advertised in *The Monthly Magazine*, Vol. 8, London: Richard Phillips, 1799.

93. This is an unjust accusation, as William Nicholson Junior is recalling just one of many experiments that were performed with a voltaic pile by Nicholson and Carlisle. Nicholson's own report of the experiment in the *Journal of Natural Philosophy, Chemistry and the Arts*, July 1800, explains how on 30 April 1800 'Mr Carlisle had provided a pile consisting of 17 half-crowns, with a like number of pieces of zinc, and of pasteboard, soaked in salt water', and how they both contributed to a series of experiments with the voltaic pile over the next few days.

94. William Stodart (1792–1838), of 1 Golden Square, patented the upright piano.

95. Alessandro Volta (1745–1827), Italian physicist, built the first continuous supply of electricity through a process of converting chemical energy via a pile of metallic discs. He published his results in 1799, but news reached England only in April 1800.

amusement and afterwards lent it to my father. At the end of a long form in the studio (the front room to the left of the door at 10 Soho Square) my father placed the washing basin half full of water, Stodart's pile standing on his right hand side when he had his back to the windows. Carlisle came in, as it appeared to me, by accident and stood at my father's right hand, I on his left. On introducing the two wires into the water in the basin my father immediately noticed the emission of gas from the extremity of each wire. The smell of hydrogen is one easily perceived, and the process of decomposition of water was at once evident to my father.

This event naturally gave rise to a conversation between Carlisle and my father, and this led to a repetition of the experiment in a bent tube or inverted siphon, by which arrangement my father was able to keep the two gases separate and perform the experiment more accurately. The consequences of this discovery were most important, and it is well known that they led to – or were the foundation of – all of Sir Humphry Davy's subsequent brilliant discoveries in the decomposition of the alkalis.[96] But my good friend Carlisle had no more to do with it than Dr Ure had in the arrangement of my father's *Dictionary of Chemistry* which he has the impudence to call his own.

On our removing to Soho Square I was getting an active boy, and here I made my first friendships with men who would not have noticed me at an earlier age. About this period the Royal Institution was established,[97] and a Dr Beddoes, who used to visit

---

96. Sir Humphry Davy, baronet (1778–1829), chemist and inventor who used the voltaic pile and the technique of electrolysis to discover or prove nine elements: sodium, boron, potassium, magnesium, calcium, barium, strontium, chlorine and iodine. He moved to London in 1801 to lecture on chemistry at the Royal Institution, having already contributed seven papers to Nicholson's *Journal*. He was knighted in 1812 and became a baronet in 1818.

97. The Royal Institution was set up in 1799 by Benjamin Thompson, Count Rumford and Sir Joseph Banks for 'diffusing the Knowledge, and Facilitating the General Introduction, of Useful Mechanical Inventions and Improvements: and for Teaching, by courses of Philosophical Lectures and Experiments, the Application of Science to the Common Purpose of Life'.

at our house, was appointed as Chemical Lecturer[98]. He was a remarkably mild and gentlemanly man.

Mr John Sadler was the Chemical Assistant.[99] This John Sadler was the son of a gentleman[100] whom William Windham,[101] the then Secretary for War under Mr Pitt, employed to construct and carry out some scheme of flying artillery which Mr Windham considered would be an improvement in warfare.

Sadler senior had a house near the park gates at Pimlico with a large piece of waste land at the back and a workshop where the various forms of flying artillery were constructed and arranged. Sadler, the son, took me to this Eldorado of my boyhood occasionally, and to climb on to the small cannon and haul them about was a treat not to be forgotten.

This Sadler, who was my good friend, was a constant inmate of Soho Square and I therefore dwell on him and his adventures. He was one of those clever, slovenly, good-natured fellows whom everyone he has met likes but whom no one calls Mister. He was essentially Jack Sadler. He was then a powerful young man of about twenty-five, and I was a boy of fifteen.

He had a great knowledge of theatrical affairs and explained to us how the transformations were managed in the pantomimes in which Bologna and Grimaldi used to cut such a figure in those

---

98. Thomas Beddoes (1760–1808) never worked at the Royal Institution but founded the Medical Pneumatic Institution in Bristol where Davy had been employed. This should refer to Dr Thomas Garnett (1766–1802), a physician and natural philosopher. He was appointed to the Royal Institution in October 1799 but resigned after a short period.

99. John Sadler (1779–1838), chemist and metallurgist.

100. John's father was James Sadler (1753–1828), chemist and the first English aeronaut to ascend in a hot-air balloon, in 1784. He made a number of improvements to weaponry and was the inventor of a horse-drawn armoured car with two small mounted cannons, known as 'Sadler's Flying Artillery'. He worked with Thomas Beddoes at the Medical Pneumatic Institution in Bristol, which may account for Nicholson Junior's confusion between Beddoes and Garnett.

101. William Windham (1750–1810), politician.

days[102]. Some of these transformations we made in pasteboard, under his tuition of course. Then he was a performer himself, being very great in the clown's dance which was then performed in a white dress with sleeves hanging down twice too long for the arms, the face painted, of course. Public masquerades were then common, and I rather think my friend had the entry into most of them, for on more than one occasion he took me to the Pantheon in Oxford Street which was preparing for an occasion of that sort. There he talked as a man in authority and showed me the mystery of the harlequin's leap through a cottage window which he could perform himself as well as any man.

As soon as Sadler was installed at the Royal Institution we heard a great deal of the gossip of the place, among other things that Count Rumford,[103] who was chief in command of the establishment which I believe he projected, used to bully poor Dr Beddoes out of his senses so that Sadler and the other under-strappers called the Count 'Old Hatchet Face' as he never came among them without having a cut at someone. Nevertheless Count Rumford, if not the originator of the Royal Institution, did good service in his day.[104] There is no question of his talent and ability, but he was a martinet where he had the power and Sadler used to say he killed poor Dr Beddoes.[105]

Then there was Accum the chemist[106], a little good-tempered German with teeth as black as ink. He came in and out of our

---

102. John Peter Bologna (1775–1846), an Italian tumbler, dancer and choreographer who came to England as a teenager with his family troupe and quickly became a famous harlequin. Joseph Grimaldi (1778–1837), an English actor, comedian and dancer, was famous for his whiteface makeup. They started to work together in 1803, performing extensively at venues such as Sadler's Wells and Covent Garden.

103. Sir Benjamin Thompson, Count Rumford (1753–1815), natural philosopher and philanthropist who promoted the Royal Institution.

104. There was, and continues to be, a debate about the precise role of Rumford in the establishment of the Royal Institution and whether he deserves credit as a founder or merely as an early administrator.

105. As in footnote 98, this should probably read Dr Garnett.

106. Friedrich Christian Accum (1769–1838), German chemist.

house just as he pleased and was a capital flute player which we boys greatly applauded as far superior to any of our performances, though we all were pipers.

In the early lectures at the Royal Institution Accum usually stood beside the lecturer with his hair powdered, and, as our friend Jack Sadler used to say, he looked like a cauliflower; which was quite true. My recollection of these early lectures, which we sometimes attended, is a lecture room three parts full with a very fashionable and inattentive audience and the door opening every ten minutes to admit one or more perfect dandies who stood with a hat on and stared about through quizzing glasses on the end of their riding whips. So far did this intrusion go that a notice was placed on the door requesting gentlemen to take off their hats on entering the lecture room, and our friend Jack Sadler suggested an addition to request them to keep on their breeches. But certainly a real dandy of those days was as rude and ill-mannered a personage as I have ever encountered.

Accum afterwards opened a shop for the sale of chemical apparatus in Compton Street and had a laboratory at the back where he lectured to a set of students. Alluding to his black teeth, he told us that he was in the habit of tasting every chemical compound and that he could detect copper in a solution when you could not precipitate it by the most delicate tests.

He wrote several useful books, one called *There Is Death in the Pot*,[107] in which he detects poison in almost all foods, and a very valuable work of chemical tests. But finally he ruined himself and had to quit the country, in consequence of having mutilated books in the library of the Royal Institution to which he had access. These books he quoted in his own works; too idle to copy, he cut out the leaves in a perfect set of my father's philosophical *Journal*. He was a cheerful, clever little fellow, and we boys were sorry to lose him.

---

107. Friedrich Accum, *There Is Death in the Pot: Treatise on Adulterations of Food and Culinary Poisons*, London: Longman, Hurst, Rees, Orme and Brown, 1820.

TO RETURN TO MY FRIEND JACK SADLER, he not only took me to Mr Windham's artillery works at Pimlico but also to a mechanical friend who was making a model steam engine. They jointly promised to make and give me a small gun, which never came to pass – and here I would remark on the cruelty of such promises and the lies they lead to.

Whenever I saw Jack Sadler, of course, I enquired of my gun. First the gun was not quite finished, next the workman was ill and then it could not be done for a month, but it never came and never was intended to come. I can remember my anxiety about this gun to this day and think of the wrong people do to children in making such promises which are never intended to be performed.

But Jack Sadler's ventures were really remarkable. First he volunteered to go, with some of Mr Windham's flying artillery, to an expedition under the Duke of York and had a narrow escape with his life.[108] He told us many amusing adventures; how he got behind an embankment and made a clay head on which he stuck his cap and feathers for the enemy to fire at while he crawled carefully some thirty yards down the ditch and made himself a loophole for his rifle and fired away in safety.

On one occasion at our house he was assisting my father in the laboratory we had and took a drink of sulphuric acid, which happened to be standing by in a pint basin close at hand. Carlisle was sent for, and the accident was got over in the best way it could be.

He next observed the red light produced by burning nitrate of strontium and thought it applicable to scenic effect. With my father's introduction to Mr Harris, then the joint proprietor of Covent Garden Theatre, he was able to introduce it for the first time in some pantomime on the stage, to his profit.

---

108. Flying artillery was taken in the Anglo-Russian invasion of Holland in 1799, led by Prince Frederick, Duke of York and Albany (1763–1827).

About this time Jack Sadler undertook the superintendence of some lead smelting works at Dukesfield near Hexham in Northumberland. The property belonged to Colonel Beaumont,[109] and it was thought that Sadler's chemical knowledge might lead to some improvement in the smelting process: which to some extent I believe it did.

On leaving London Sadler promised to send for me to visit him in the summer, which promise he kept better than the gun affair, and about midsummer I left London on my first journey of any importance and arrived at Newcastle, where Sadler met me with a horse to ride to Dukesfield. I remember I tried to get up on the wrong side of the horse, to the amusement of the bystanders.

My father had given me a letter of introduction to a bookseller in the marketplace at Newcastle, who was very kind and took me about the town and to a museum, where I have a distinct recollection of having seen over the door a stuffed bird which I was told was a dodo. It was a dingy-white colour and something about the size of a goose, in a very dirty, dilapidated condition; it seemed put on the shelf as lumber. I had read all about the dodo and how the Dutch men in Mauritius had eaten them all up, so that this circumstance fixed my attention. This must have been about sixty-five years since, and now that so much is said of the want of all traces of the bird would it not be well to see what became of this old specimen?[110]

Sadler was very kind in procuring me a pony and other amusements, and after a time we set off in company with

109. Thomas Richard Beaumont (1758–1829); the property was actually inherited by his wife, Diana Beaumont (c.1765–1831), and she was the driving force behind a very profitable business.

110. On 4 October 2012 The Journal reported that while volunteers from AkzoNobel were helping to tidy the stores at the Great North Museum they discovered a long-lost dodo in the Hancock Museum collection in Newcastle (www.thejournal.co.uk/news/north-east-news/volunteers-help-great-north-museum-4401676; accessed 12 November 2017).

a neighbouring farmer to Gilsland Spa, where a large company were assembled to amuse themselves and drink mineral waters or brandy and water, as they chose.

Sadler was the life and soul of our party and, what with queer stories and comic songs, was in great request. But all good things come to an end and after a time Sadler and I and our farmer friend mounted our steeds and headed for home. At a mile or so from Gilsland Hotel the road turned in those days nearly at a right-angle over a stone bridge with very low parapet walls. Approaching the bridge we were suddenly deluged with rain, and the thunder and lightning startled Sadler's gallant grey and away we went full gallop towards the bridge, I on my pony last.

On arriving at the bridge, Sadler's horse made a dash for a leap at the parapet wall, which Sadler struggled to prevent, the horse came up all of a heap against the wall, Sadler went over his head and hung with the bridle in his hand, while the horse was struggling on the bridge. At length Sadler let go, or the rein broke, just at the very moment that the torrent rushed over the limestone bed of the brook and saved him from certain destruction. The fall was between sixteen and eighteen feet, and a minute before there was not a drop of water on the stony bed of the brook.

The horse struggling away, with the reins held by Sadler, had managed to pull down the coping of the parapet, some of which pitched on his off forefoot, and he went limping away. Our farmer waded into the water and got Sadler out, and I galloped back to the inn for aid.

Every gentleman at table turned out, and we soon had Sadler conveyed back in an open carriage, bruised and shaken but with only a wound on the shin of the right leg. He soon recovered, and I left him hearty and well at Dukesfield when I came away, but this was one of the break-neck adventures which were constantly befalling my friend.

Jack Sadler's father and his brother, Windham Sadler, had often made ascensions in balloons, and poor Windham Sadler was ultimately killed from a balloon at Blackburn. Prior to this misfortune, Windham Sadler had made thirty-two ascents and on one occasion passed from Dublin to Wales.

The ascents in which Jack Sadler occasionally assisted gave him some knowledge of balloons, and he undertook an ascent himself on the occasion of some public fête. This adventure, like the last, had nearly proved fatal. As I have heard him describe it, it must have been very alarming.

He had reached considerable altitude on a tolerably calm day and was nearly over the woods in Kensington Gardens when he observed the car in which he stood gradually receding from the body of the balloon; he immediately concluded that the network that enclosed the balloon and by which the car was suspended must be imperfect or loose at the top of the balloon. Indeed it was clear that the body of the balloon was gradually slipping out of the network.

The first thing he did was to seize the tube or pipe that hung down from the lower end of the balloon and wind it fast round his arm so as to relieve the car of his weight, and thus he continued to ascend higher and higher. The car, however, though relieved of his weight continued to fall from his feet, and he and the balloon seemed likely to go alone. Thus hanging by one arm he sought in his pockets for a knife, which he fortunately found, and cut as far as he could into the balloon. The escape of gas half stifled him, but his escape was secured, and he landed on earth more dead than alive after this strange adventure.

But what I relate is only part of the adventures of Jack Sadler who eventually found a resting place with Mr Beaufoy,[111] son

---

111. Henry Benjamin Hanbury Beaufoy (1786–1851) inherited the Beaufoy distillery in Lambeth, which produced gin, vinegar and wines. In 1849 he built the Ragged School for Boys and Girls in Newport Street.

of Colonel Beaufoy, at some chemical works in which he was interested. I always look back on him (now dead and gone) as an extraordinary character and a very clever fellow.

The strontium light gave Jack Sadler the entrée to the theatre, where he often took me. I specifically recall seeing Mrs Siddons,[112] John[113] and Charles Kemble,[114] Incledon[115] as well as Braham[116] at the zenith of his fame.

When Philidor first produced the Phantasmagoria at the Lyceum Theatre in the Strand,[117] we were at one of the earliest performances. The effect was very striking and wonderful to me, but Sadler soon detected how it was done, and after it was over we called on his friend Charles Dibdin the Younger[118] and told him all we had seen. Dibdin, being a dramatist and familiar with theatrical affairs, immediately proposed (if Sadler was sure he could do it) to go into the provinces with this performance before anyone else started. Dibdin could leave London and he proposed introducing some theatrical acquaintance of which the Phantasmagoria was to be the main feature. This gentleman, whom we met afterwards at Dibdin's lodging, was a poor sort of player and proposed the recital of poetry, by himself, to fill up the entertainment.

To give us a touch of his quality, he got up and repeated 'The Three Warnings'[119] in a most melancholy style. The drift of the poem was that Death had a call on Mr Dobson, who complained of the want of warning. So Death walked off and did not come

---

112. Sarah Siddons, née Kemble (1755–1831), actress.

113. John Kemble (1757–1823), actor.

114. Charles Kemble (1775–1854), actor and dramatist.

115. Charles Incledon (c.1763–1826), singer.

116. John Braham (c.1777–1856), singer.

117. Paul Philidor (d.1829) set up the *Phantasmagoria* exhibition at the Lyceum Theatre in London in 1801, combining theatrics with scientific effects and demonstrations of automata. He later went into partnership with Marie Tussaud.

118. Charles Isaac Mungo Dibdin (1768–1833), dramatist.

119. Written in 1766 by Hester Lynch Thrale Piozzi (1741–1821).

again for some time. The next time he came, Mr Dobson made the same excuse of want of warning, but Death reminded him he was deaf and nearly blind, which with some other small ailments he considered a fair warning, so he carried him off. This as a prologue to an exhibition of spectres and deaths' heads in the dark seemed rather too sad, and the negotiation fell to the ground.

During my father's residence in Soho Square, which lasted from about 1800 to 1810, we generally had eight or ten young gentlemen studying under my father and various masters, to whom my father delivered a lecture on natural philosophy once a week. In these lectures Jack Sadler was, as usual, the assistant.

At the same time my father gave a public course of twelve lectures, he was consulted daily on scientific subjects, and he undertook the office of engineer to the West Middlesex Water Works[120] where Mr Millington was clerk of the works.[121] In addition, he held a *conversazione* every Tuesday night where eight or ten gentlemen generally attended to discuss the literature and science of the day.[122] Among the attendants on these evenings were Carlisle, Dr Buchan,[123] Dr Combe, the pianoforte manufacturers Lewis and Willard, Sir Humphry Davy and Dr Cochran.

These various occupations certainly brought him an ample revenue, but unfortunately there were ample means of dissipating such revenue. My father, fully occupied, seldom left his study or laboratory but to his meals or on business calls, and as I have before said was the least worldly man I have ever met with.

---

120. Established in 1806.

121. John Millington (1779–1868) was chief engineer for West Middlesex Water Works for twenty-five years and lectured at the Royal Institution on natural philosophy from 1815.

122. To be held every Wednesday, from the first Wednesday in November 1799 to the last Wednesday in June 1800, advertised in *The Monthly Magazine*, Vol. 8, London: Richard Phillips, 1799.

123. Dr William Buchan (1729–1805), physician and author of *Domestic Medicine: or, a Treatise on the Prevention and Cure of Diseases by Regimen and Simple Medicines*, one of the best-selling books of its kind.

Thus all domestic affairs were left to my mother, who with six grown-up daughters and I and my brothers at school dissipated every farthing of revenue.

I have often conversed with gentlemen in later life who had been pupils of my father's, and we invariably agree that the house in Soho Square was an establishment to which we have never met with anything similar for thoughtless hospitality and reckless expenditure. My brother and I were too young to observe or to have any control. My father, constantly occupied, left all to my mother who, though the kindest and best of parents, had not the remotest idea of care or economy.

As one example of management, Carlisle told me that he had seen six hackney coaches at our door during one morning, for the various members of the family to drive in their various ways to visit their friends and acquaintances. Then whoever called would be invited to stay to dinner or to our evening parties, and that large house was always full of company and every bed occupied. Breakfast was going forward from nine o'clock till noon, then a dinner of fifteen or twenty people, tea and then a party, the opera, play or other amusement.

In all this my father was too busy a man to participate and was generally writing in his study while the company were singing duets in the drawing-room.

The fame of 10 Soho Square spread far and wide, and not a ship from Madras or Calcutta arrived without bringing one or more visitors. These were chiefly young officers introduced by gentlemen who had entered the army or the Civil Service after having been pupils at my father's house, and all were welcome.

I name these domestic affairs to explain why my father, who by his sole labour commanded so handsome a revenue, was always a comparatively poor man.

In 1809 my father published *The British Encyclopedia, or Dictionary of Arts and Sciences: Comprising an Accurate and Popular View of the Present Improved State of Human Knowledge* in six octavo volumes. This was the last work of any importance my father published, the preface dated 21 December 1808. He was assisted by various gentlemen who are all acknowledged in the preface to the work with the various subjects they wrote on.

Among them were Peter Nicholson[124] on architecture and Charles Sylvester of Derby[125] on galvanism. The latter gentleman we knew well but the former, though of our name, was no relation.

Mr Sylvester had the misfortune to have lost some of his fingers, and I remember him going into the shop of a simple woman and asking for a pair of gloves. Looking over the gloves, he asked the good woman if she had any with two fingers, showing her his hand. Of course she had none. He showed her a pair of which he had pulled the wanting fingers into the glove and said they would do; taking his money, she remarked that she really did not know she had such a pair of gloves in her stock. Sylvester delighted in these simple jokes and was always an amusing companion and a favourite wherever he was.

My father, though much assistance was derived from others, wrote upwards of two hundred articles on chemistry, natural philosophy and mechanics, besides the lives of many eminent men.

───────◆───────

124. Peter Nicholson (1765–1844), architectural author and mathematician.
125. Charles Sylvester (1774–1828), chemist and inventor.

FTER 1808 MY FATHER'S ATTENTION WAS MAINLY DIRECTED TOWARDS ENGINEERING PROJECTS rather than authorship, and the success of the West Middlesex Water Works led him to turn his attention to other towns which were wanting the needful supply. I have Cary's map of England, on which he has carefully drawn a coloured circle around every town; the colours are referred to in the margin as indicating the number of houses in each town. At length he decided on Portsmouth, which was at that period supplied by water carts.

My father took me with him to Portsmouth to reconnoitre the place early in 1808, and I remember starting from the Golden Cross, Charing Cross, my father inside and I outside, which I thought more manly. We had a telescope and a small pocket sextant for taking angles, and the day after our arrival we went about to make a rough survey of the place and gain what information we could.

Using the sextant and occasionally looking through the telescope together, with our being strangers we soon attracted attention, and our movements were reported to the authorities. The following morning an official waited on my father at the inn with a request to attend some meeting of those in authority.

I rather think it was a military meeting, as Portsmouth was a military town. I of course waited at the inn and on my father's return learned that all had turned out for the best.

Many of the gentlemen knew my father's name from his writings, and all approved of the object of his visit. He also learned the drainage of the town was very imperfect, so much so that soldiers had been known to faint and fall out of ranks on parade from the stench of the sewage. This deficiency in the drainage was in consequence of the want of fall in these flat localities and is experienced in Hull and elsewhere to this day. My father suggested flushing the drains with water periodically, which met with their general approval.

At this period the water carts got their supply for the town from a spring on Southsea Common near at hand, and, as there was no river or fresh water stream in reach of Portsmouth, the proposed supply on an enlarged scale was necessarily restricted to this source.

The geological formation of this district had been so thoroughly investigated, even at this period, by John Farey the elder[126] and others, that there was little difficulty in determining whence the water was supplied through the chalk formation which cropped out at the point on the Southsea Common where the spring is situated, and my father rather astonished a meeting of proprietors in the proposed undertaking by stating that the whole supply of water came from the Isle of Wight, which in fact it does. The chalk formation dips in nearly a semi-circular curve under the arm of the sea which divides the island from the mainland, rising again at the point and afterwards forming Portsdown Hill and the continuous chalk formation into the heart of Hampshire.

With boring and other aids to augment the discharge of water at this old spring, the supply was found adequate and works were erected and Portsmouth abundantly supplied with good water ever since.[127]

Gosport, a town on the other side of the harbour, was next undertaken and then the borough of Southwark, in both of which, as well as in the Portsmouth Company, my father held a considerable interest as well as receiving a salary for engineering. The first was not so successful, but the second I believe answered well.

---

126. John Farey (1766–1826), geologist and surveyor.
127. The Company of the Proprietors of the Portsea Island Water Works, (the Portsea Island Company) was established in 1809 and first piped water to the residents of Portsmouth on 29 April 1811.

A BOUT THIS TIME, I LEFT MY FATHER'S HOUSE to attend to business affairs on my own account, and my younger brother remained with my father as his assistant. I am not therefore so well acquainted with the details of his affairs hereafter.

It is clear that my father's constant absence from home on these various projects and increasing engagements as a consulting engineer would leave his pupils in Soho Square rather neglected, and when I left home there were no fresh ones applying. The young gentlemen who were there were necessarily leaving periodically, and thus that part of my father's vocation gradually died a natural death.

In March 1809 Holcroft died, and I remember there was a post-mortem examination by Carlisle and Dr Buchan.

Carlisle had been knighted by this time, and Sir Anthony Carlisle had been called in to see the Prince Regent[128], mainly to consult as to what wine he should drink. Having ascertained that brown sherry was the favourite of the day, he recommended it and gave great satisfaction.

Carlisle wrote to me, while I was engaged in a survey in Yorkshire, to find him a handy, honest, unsophisticated lad as a servant. I did my best and sent him one. The lad turned out a stupid dog, but when I visited London a short time afterwards and dined with Carlisle this boy waited and amused me by incessantly answering Carlisle, 'Yes, Sir Anthony... no, Sir Anthony' and 'Sir Anthony' at the beginning, middle and end of every sentence. All this passed as a matter of course and reminded me how calmly we bear our dignities when they fall upon us.

Carlisle was a true fisherman and a great admirer of honest Izaak Walton[129] and used to quote from that delightful book *The Compleat Angler*, so that when any food or wine was better than

---

128. Carlisle was Surgeon Extraordinaire to King George IV between 1820 and 1830. He was knighted in 1821.

129. Izaak Walton (1593–1683), writer and fly-fisherman.

common he said it was only fit for anglers or very honest men; and then he had another joke when we got thoroughly wet on our fishing excursions, saying it was a discovery, how to wash your feet without taking off your stockings.

Sir Joseph Banks, who resided at number 32 Soho Square, at that time held weekly soirées at which my father was a pretty constant attendant. Although my father admitted the claims of the great naturalist, he always had a feeling that Sir Joseph had not done him justice. The main point on which my father felt aggrieved was his rejection at the Royal Society. My father had been recommended by several of the members of the Society to offer himself. He was duly proposed but objected to.

It came to my father's ears that Sir Joseph Banks was the chief objector, having said that whatever pretensions Mr Nicholson had to the membership he did not think a 'sailor boy' a fit person to rank among the gentlemen members of the Royal Society, or words to that effect.

That the allusion to my father's early vocation as a 'sailor boy' had been made on this occasion is pretty certain in my mind as I heard Carlisle, Dr Buchan and Dr Combe allude to it in a joking way when my father was spoken of, saying that 'the sailor boy had done pretty well in doing so and so . . .'

Be this as it may, my father always attended Sir Joseph's soirées, and I have heard from others that his remarkable conversational powers and great attainments and amiable placid way of expressing his opinion rendered him a general favourite and frequent speaker at these meetings.

I believe that Dr Solander,[130] a Swedish gentleman who had accompanied Sir Joseph round the world with Captain Cook,[131]

---

130. Daniel Solander (1733–82), botanist.
131. Joseph Banks and Daniel Solander accompanied Captain James Cook (1728–79) on the first voyage of the HMS *Endeavour* to Australia (1768–71).

was an intimate in his house. At any rate, he officiated as a sort of secretary at these meetings and found any book of reference that might be required and seems to have directed the proceedings.

My father frequently reproved us for lolling on any book when reading and used to say, 'When Dr Solander brings a book to any gentleman, he will immediately speak if the book is used carelessly.' Thus he himself had placed his hand on the leaf of a book to keep it open, when Dr Solander touched him gently on the shoulder and said the book would keep open of itself. The rough and careless manner in which some people use books fully justifies these rebukes.

There was a widow lady, who lived in a rather fashionable style near Portman Square, to whom Sir Joseph Banks was a guardian or in trust in some way, and her son was a pupil with my father. I often accompanied the son on a visit to his mother, who was very kind to me, and on more than one occasion she took me in her carriage to call on Sir Joseph, who joined us in the carriage and drove to the Bank of England, where I presume they went to draw dividends or transact other business. On one occasion he wore a blue ribbon, and we left him at St James's, where I conclude he was going to Court[132]. My recollection of him is of a burly good-tempered man, but I as a boy was taken little notice of.

Sir Humphry Davy, then Mr Davy, was occasionally at my father's, and since my father's death I have found some notes from him to my father respecting appointments to meet on consultations on chemical questions which had been referred to them. He was a particularly neat person in his dress at that time, and my recollection is of a very reserved person, but then this impression might arise from my being so much younger.

Count Rumford called but seldom.

---

132. Banks was invested as a Knight of the Order of the Bath on 1 July 1795. On 4 July a cartoon called *The Great South Sea Caterpillar*, by the caricaturist James Gillray, was published showing Banks wearing the blue ribbon and the jewel of Bath.

T HERE WAS ONE PERSON that sought my father who I should have thought the least likely of any man to do so. This was Thomas Pitt, 2nd Baron Camelford,[133] who was afterwards shot in a duel with Captain Best near Holland House.[134] How Camelford became known to my father or he to him I never knew, and as the business which brought them together had nothing to do with either science or art I am the more surprised.

Lord Camelford had determined to purchase two ships and fit them out in the best style and with all modern appliances for the South Sea Whale Fishery, and he fixed on my father to aid him in carrying out his project. Lord Camelford was constantly at our house in consultation, but all the detail rested with my father; who applied to Mr Rogers,[135] a reputable merchant in the City, to find the ships.

My father and I accompanied Mr Rogers in the examination of a great number in the river and docks, and what struck me as remarkable was the minute inventory of the various vessels' belongings, which generally ranged from the chain cable and anchor to three pewter spoons and a mustard pot, etc. In a ship costing many thousands this seemed to me very odd.

Two ships were bought, the one called *The Experiment* having something novel in her construction; the name of the other I have forgotten.

Both ships were properly equipped, captains engaged by Mr Rogers, and they sailed for the South Seas to capture whales. The

133. Thomas Pitt, 2nd Baron Camelford (1775–1804), described as an 'uncertified lunatic' and 'the half-mad Lord'. He contributed £1,500 to the establishment of Nicholson's school in Soho Square. The connection is not so surprising when you consider that the membership of the Society for the Improvement of Naval Architecture included a couple of Camelford's relations.

134. Holland House was once the largest private residence in London, surrounded by countryside in 1804 when it was the headquarters of the Whig Party and famous for its social gatherings.

135. Isaac Rogers (c.1754–c.1839) of 24 Little Bell Alley, a member of the Society for the Improvement of Naval Architecture.

ships had not long been gone when Lord Camelford got into the unfortunate dispute with Captain Best which led to the fatal duel.

They met in a field at the back of Holland House; where Cromwell held his council, Addison died, and poor Sheridan used to get so drunk. There Lord Camelford, a young athlete and highly educated man, was shot through the vertebrae and the lower extremities were completely paralysed, in which miserable condition he lingered a while and then died.

My father saw him several times as he lay in this sad condition, and everything was done that could be done under the circumstances to put the whale fishing speculation in as clear a matter of account as could be. Nevertheless, Lord Camelford's relatives or those who succeeded to the management of his estate blamed my father for leading him into the enterprise.

Nothing could be further from the truth. Is it at all likely that my father, an elderly and studious man, should seek a young man of fashion whose pursuits were diametrically opposite to his own to propose a whale-catching adventure? No, Lord Camelford sought him, and why he should think him a fit agent for such an undertaking I own is past my comprehension.

From all that I could ever gather respecting this extraordinary transaction, it appears that Lord Camelford had persuaded himself that Bonaparte,[136] who was then carrying all before him on the Continent, would ultimately conquer England and that it was a wise policy to sell real property and invest your means in more portable securities. Then his coming to my father must have arisen from the recommendation of some of the fashionable young men who have been my father's pupils, but this is a mere guess.

Old Rogers – we always called him that – seems to have picked up two complete scoundrels as captains, and all went very wrong,

---

136. Napoleon Bonaparte (1769–1821), French military and political leader who became the first Emperor of the French in December 1804.

and ultimately serious loss was incurred. Rogers was a very old friend of my father's, a well-to-do city merchant, a bachelor who lived in an old-fashioned mansion in Bell Alley at the back of the Bank of England. Here we went once a year to a grand feast, my father, mother and all the available children.

The provision was sumptuous in our eyes, and after dinner we boys and girls were allowed to look into a long closet sort of room, with a window at the end, which was a sort of museum. There were clubs and dresses worked with beads and shells from the South Sea Islands, model canoes and two or three hideous heads from Borneo. But near the window was the most beautiful model of a first-rate man-of-war I ever saw before or since. It was a full five feet long, full rigged and complete in every particular. It must have cost many hundreds of pounds, and it was housed in a glass case which pulled up by a counter weight, like a window sash. When Old Rogers thought we had had time to be satisfied with the clubs and skulls, he came and raised the glass and showed us the first step of the ladder leading from the quarter-deck to the poop on which Lord Howe sat on 1 June 1794 at the battle with the French off Ushant, dressed in sailor's uniform to avoid being a mark for the enemy.[137]

After this was seen and explained the museum faded away and was forgotten until the next annual meeting, then tea and home in a glass coach, which a hired coach without a number was called in those days.

---

137. The Battle of the 'Glorious First' of June in 1794 was the first naval conflict during the French Revolutionary Wars. It sought to prevent a convoy of ships carrying grain from reaching France. The weather on 1 June was 'glorious' and gave the British fleet the advantage, such that 7000 French sailors were killed, wounded and captured compared with just 1000 British sailors killed or wounded.

ANOTHER NOBLEMAN, THE CELEBRATED LORD COCHRANE,[138] was frequently in consultation with my father, but his was a more legitimate business than the last lord's. He was both a chemist and a mechanic and a man of considerable scientific attainments in every department. He took out several patents for his various inventions; one for a street lamp was thought a great improvement, and I know my father thought very highly of many improvements and inventions he suggested. He was a powerful, tall man and remarkably gentlemanly and courteous.

About 1809 I left my father's house to undertake the survey and management of some estates in Yorkshire belonging to the Right Honourable Henry Lord Middleton,[139] and my younger brother, John,[140] remained with my father as his main assistant.

Shortly after this time my father removed to a larger house on the west side of Bloomsbury Square. Here he continued his engineering and other pursuits and was daily consulted by the whole world of science of the period; and the domestic doings equalled or eclipsed the fame of Soho Square.

Indeed whatever revenue my poor father's laborious habits and indomitable energy might command, there were adequate demands in a family of ten or twelve grown-up people, adequate servants and a house like a caravansary.[141]

Speaking with a titled gentleman some years ago, then high in the Government and living in the splendour of the fashionable world, we referred to Soho Square where he had formerly studied with my father; and he remarked, 'Well, of all the houses I ever

---

138. Archibald Cochrane, 9th Earl of Dundonald (1748–1831), chemist and industrialist.

139. Lord Henry Middleton (1761–1835). This estate is probably Birdsall House in Malton, North Yorkshire, where Thomas Willoughby took shelter in a snowstorm in and fell in love with the heiress, Elizabeth Sotheby, whom he married.

140. John Nicholson (b. 1791), author of *The Operative Mechanic, and British Machinist*, printed for Knight and Lacey, 1825.

141. A type of inn, found in the Middle East, with a large central courtyard where travellers with camels could stop for the night.

knew, I never knew one where money was so swattered away[142] as it was there.' This was about the truth, no fault of my father, who was much from home and constantly occupied; but the consequences were to be painfully recognized when he got old and ailing and was no longer able to pursue with energy his former pursuits.

He left Bloomsbury Square for a house in Charlotte Street, Bloomsbury, where he died in 1815. My brother remained with him to the last, and Carlisle attended him. He had drunk nothing except water since he was twenty years of age and drank so freely of water that Carlisle always said it was partly the cause of his ailment, which was an affliction of the kidneys. Born in 1753, he was sixty-one years of age.[143]

———◆———

142. 'Splashed around'.
143. William Nicholson died on the morning of Sunday 21 May, 1815. He was buried on 23 May in St George's Burial Grounds, Bloomsbury, one of the earliest burial grounds to be established at a distance from its church, due to the growing problem of overcrowding. Today, gravestones rest against the walls of St George's Gardens in the London Borough of Camden where, sadly, most are illegible after years of erosion.

'The hypothesis of this learned and laborious philosopher . . . is very ingenious indeed.'

— Alessandro Volta, writing to Sir Joseph Banks, on the subject of Nicholson's article about the torpedo fish[144], 1800.[145]

---

144. William Nicholson, 'Observations on the Electrophore, Tending to Explain the Means by which the Torpedo and Other Fish Communicate the Electric Shock', *A Journal of Natural Philosophy, Chemistry and the Arts*, November 1797.

145. See note 4, page 13, for the full reference for this letter.

AFTERWORD

Locating William Nicholson

*By Frank A.J.L. James, Professor of the History of Science,
the Royal Institution and University College London*

William Nicholson is best remembered for two things: his founding
and editing of *A Journal of Natural Philosophy, Chemistry, and the
Arts* (universally known as Nicholson's Journal)[146] in 1797, and using
Alessandro Volta's invention of the electric pile (later called the
battery) to decompose water electrically for the first time, in 1800.[147]
These were both critically important contributions to the development
of science in the late eighteenth and early nineteenth centuries. But
that is not all, for he also contributed to developing the hydrometer,
inventing a slide rule and cylinder printing. Despite their significance,
these aspects of Nicholson's work have been eclipsed by his editing
and electrical researches.

The memoir, published here for the first time, written by his
son more than fifty years after Nicholson's death, illustrates his
involvement in London's rich scientific culture, though the text is
not properly chronological nor always accurate. Nevertheless, the
memoir is extraordinarily evocative of the social world of scientific
London in the 1790s and early nineteenth century, with its small clubs,

146. .*Nicholson's Journal* has been discussed in: Samuel Lilley, 'Nicholson's Journal (1797–
    1813)', *Annals of Science*, 1948, Vol. 6, pp. 78–101; Jonathan Topham, 'Anthologizing the
    Book of Nature: The Circulation of Knowledge and the Origins of the Scientific Journal
    in Late Georgian Britain', in Bernard Lightman, Gordon McOuat and Larry Stewart (eds),
    *The Circulation of Knowledge between Britain, India and China: The Early-Modern World to
    the Twentieth Century*, Leiden: Brill, 2013, pp. 119–52; Iain P. Watts, '"We want no authors":
    William Nicholson and the Contested Role of the Scientific Journal in Britain, 1797–1813',
    British Journal for the History of Science, 2014, Vol. 47, pp. 397–419.

147. Giuliano Pancaldi, *Volta: Science and Culture in the Age of Enlightenment*, Princeton:
    Princeton University Press, 2005, pp. 212–18, 228–30.

aristocratic patronage, radical politics, book trade, consequences of the long war against France (including foreign spies and military preparations) and much else besides. It is against this background that Nicholson's lasting scientific contributions emerged and came to be defined.

It is clear from the memoir and from other sources that Nicholson, like many connected with the book trade at the time, was involved in the radical political discussions of 1790s London.[148] For instance, following his return from serving as Wedgwood's agent in the Netherlands in the late 1770s, Nicholson lodged with the playwright Thomas Holcroft, who later become one of the leading English Jacobins, strongly supporting the French Revolution. He was charged with treason in 1794, but never tried because others with similar views were acquitted and the government wished to avoid further embarrassment. Through Holcroft, Nicholson became acquainted with John Thelwall (tried but acquitted for treason) and, above all, with William Godwin. Godwin first noted Nicholson in his diary towards the end of 1788 and thereafter Nicholson figures prominently for the remainder of his life. Indeed, there is a significant peak in references to Nicholson in the diary in the period leading up to the publication in February 1793 of Godwin's seminal *Enquiry Concerning Political Justice*. Nicholson drafted an obituary of Godwin's wife in 1797, the author Mary Wollstonecraft[149] and undertook a phrenological study of their three-week-old daughter, the future Mary Shelley.[150]

As the Revolution turned to Terror and ultimately to military dictatorship, many of Nicholson's literary associates were English

148. For example, Richard Taylor or George Riebau. See respectively W.H. Brock and A.J. Meadows, *The Lamp of Learning: Taylor and Francis and the Development of Science Publishing* (2nd edn), London: Taylor and Francis, 1998) and Frank A.J.L. James, *Michael Faraday: A Very Short Introduction*, Oxford: Oxford University Press, 2010.

149. Bodleian MS Abinger c.3, f.115–16.

150. William Nicholson to William Godwin, 18 September 1797, Charles Kegan Paul, *William Godwin: His Friends and Contemporaries* (2 volumes), London: Henry S. King and Co., 1876, Vol. 1, pp. 289–90.

Jacobins and would have been seen as what one author, Kenneth Johnston, has called 'Unusual Suspects' which include Godwin and Thelwall. Nicholson is not in the index of Johnston's book[151], which suggests that his ability to distance himself politically was more effective than that of his colleagues.

Nevertheless, for those in the know, such distancing would, at least in the short to medium term, be ineffective and this probably accounts for the comparative historical neglect accorded to Nicholson, apart from his two major contributions which could scarcely be overlooked.

Despite publishing three papers in the *Philosophical Transactions* in the 1780s, Nicholson was never elected to Fellowship of the Royal Society of London, which might reasonably have been expected. Although Nicholson knew the society's president, Joseph Banks, and indeed for a while lived near him in Soho Square, attending his soirées, the memoir blames Banks for blocking the nomination explicitly on the class grounds that Nicholson was a 'sailor boy', having in his youth served as a midshipman in the service of the East India Company. While this may well have been the reason, another possible motive could have been Nicholson's politics, which Banks would have abhorred.

It was in the charged and constantly changing political atmosphere of the 1790s that Nicholson decided in 1797 to establish his *Journal*, which would be a commercially published monthly scientific periodical. Along with the establishment of small scientific discussion groups or clubs, such as the Coffee House Philosophical Society, the London Mineralogical Society, the Askesian Society, the Geological Society, the City Philosophical Society, the Philosophical Society of London, the Chemical Club and so on, new periodicals were also founded during this period of war against France. In addition to

---

151. Kenneth R. Johnston, *Unusual Suspects: Pitt's Reign of Alarm and the Lost Generation of the 1790s*, Oxford: Oxford University Press, 2013.

Nicholson's Journal, these included *The Philosophical Magazine* and *The Director*. These societies and journals had mixed success, some surviving to this day, most not. What they all had in common was a sense of dissatisfaction with the Royal Society of London under Banks's leadership.

Nicholson explicitly modelled his *Journal* on existing Continental examples[152] including the *Journal de Physique* (founded 1773), the *Annales de Chimie* (1789) and the *Journal der Physik* (1790),[153] as well as some British predecessors such as the *Repertory of Arts and Manufactures* (1794),[154] with the aim of including the work of those outside the Royal Society of London élites and with much faster publication than possible with the twice-yearly *Philosophical Transactions*. Initially sales were slow, which Nicholson attributed to general wartime distress,[155] but reportedly within ten years *Nicholson's Journal* had reached an impressive circulation of one thousand.[156] Content was varied and it was the second highest cited journal in the eighth edition of William Henry's *Elements of Experimental Chemistry* (1818).[157] Its readership was not confined to what we would nowadays view as scientific, but included savants such as Samuel Coleridge and Robert Southey, both of whom had a serious chemical interest inspired by their close friendship with Humphry Davy, made while he was in Bristol working at the Medical Pneumatic Institution under Thomas Beddoes.

The benefits of the speedy publication of the latest scientific news in *Nicholson's Journal* is well illustrated by the dissemination

---

152. See the four-page printed advertisement dated 1 March 1797 for the journal that Nicholson produced. (Copy in the John Johnson Collection at the Bodleian.)

153. Lilley, p. 80.

154. Topham, pp. 130–33.

155. [William Nicholson] 'Advertisement', 1 March 1798, *Nicholson's Journal*, 1798, Vol. 1, p. v.

156. Watts, p. 5.

157. Lilley, p. 99. Lilley includes a useful, if somewhat old-fashioned, summary of the content of *Nicholson's Journal*.

in Britain of Volta's discovery that a pile of alternating metal discs interspersed with acidic paper or cloth produced galvanic electricity. Volta announced his invention in two letters written to Banks dated, from Como, 20 March and 1 April 1800.[158] The first letter, sent by post, arrived during April, but the second, carried by a merchant, was not received until the start of June at the earliest. This delay explains why they were not read to the Royal Society of London until 26 June 1800.[159] But Banks evidently told his acquaintances about the first letter since, according to Nicholson in the July issue of his *Journal*, Volta's discovery had been 'a subject of great attention among philosophers for near two months'[160] – that is, since April. Nicholson, with help from the surgeon Anthony Carlisle, built a pile during this period and decomposed water electrically for the first time[161], a result confirmed by the chemistry lecturer at the Royal Military Academy, Woolwich, William Cruickshank.[162]

Before the second letter arrived, the first public announcement of Volta's work and Nicholson's and Carlisle's discovery was made during a lecture delivered on Wednesday 28 May 1800 by Thomas Garnett at the Royal Institution. He borrowed apparatus from Edward Howard[163] to demonstrate Volta's discovery, which suggests that it might have come from Cruickshank with whom Howard collaborated.[164] Garnett was widely reported, in newspapers such as the *Morning Chronicle*, *The Sun* and several others, as saying that Nicholson and Carlisle had

158. Royal Society of London MS L&P/11/137, pp. 1–4 and 5–21.

159. Alessandro Volta, 'On the Electricity Excited by the Mere Contact of Conducting Substances of Different Kinds', *Philosophical Transactions*, 1800, Vol. 90, pp. 403–31.

160. William Nicholson, 'Account of the new Electrical or Galvanic Apparatus of Sig. Alex. Volta, and Experiments performed with the same', *Nicholson's Journal*, 1800, Vol. 4, pp. 179–87, p. 179.

161. Nicholson, 'Account', p. 179.

162. William Cruickshank, 'Some Experiments and Observations on Galvanic Electricity', *Nicholson's Journal*, 1800, Vol. 4, pp. 187–91.

163. Rumford to Joseph Banks, 29 May 1800, Dartmouth College, MS Rauner Rumford 800329.

164. Frederick Kurzer, 'The Life and Work of Edward Charles Howard', *Annals of Science*, 1999, Vol. 56, pp. 113–41.

repeated Volta's discovery of the electrical decomposition of water.[165] This incorrect claim drew a stinging correction from Nicholson, published in the *Morning Chronicle* and elsewhere, together with a hint that both Garnett and the Royal Institution had behaved with impropriety in announcing Volta's work before it had been read to the Royal Society of London.[166] This would doubtless have helped deflect attention from Nicholson's imminent publication (well before its appearance in *Philosophical Transactions*) of his own work, which, *inter alia*, announced Volta's discovery for the first time in a scientific journal rather than a newspaper.

Probably via the July issue of *Nicholson's Journal*, Davy in Bristol received news early that month of Volta's work and the research stemming from it undertaken by Nicholson, Carlisle and Cruickshank,[167] just in time to reference it briefly at the end of his book mostly devoted to his investigations into nitrous oxide.[168] Beddoes arranged for a pile to be built[169] and for the remainder of the year Davy experimented on galvanism. Davy recorded this research in two notebooks, beginning in August,[170] and in a series of monthly papers sent to *Nicholson's Journal* from September 1800 through to February 1801, apart from January. In these papers Davy announced, amongst other discoveries, that electricity would pass through organic tissue, that charcoal could be used as an electric pole and came to the overall conclusion, contra Volta, that 'Galvanism [was]

165. *Morning Chronicle*, 30 May 1800, 3c; *The Star*, 30 May 1800, 3c; *The Sun*, 31 May 1800, 4b; *The General Evening Post*, 29–31 May 1800, 1b; *The Whitehall Evening Post*, 29–31 May 1800, 2c; *Evening Mail*, 2–4 June 1800, 1b; *St. James's Chronicle*, 14–17 June 1800, 1d.

166. William Nicholson to the editor, 1 June 1800, *Morning Chronicle*, 3 June 1800, 3c. Also published in *The Albion and Evening Advertiser*, 3 June 1800, 3d.

167. Humphry Davy to Davies Giddy, 3 July 1800, John Ayrton Paris, *The Life of Sir Humphry Davy* (2 volumes), London: H. Colburn and R. Bentley, 1831, Vol. 1, pp. 85–8.

168. Humphry Davy, *Researches, Chemical and Philosophical; Chiefly Concerning Nitrous Oxide, or Dephlogisticated Nitrous Air, and Its Respiration*, London: J. Johnson, 1800, p. 568.

169. *Nicholson's Journal*, 1800, Vol. 4, p. 275.

170. RI MS HD/20/C and /22/B.

a process purely chemical'.[171] Thus *Nicholson's Journal* became the major conduit in English by which details of new research on voltaic electricity, especially Davy's, was disseminated.

In March 1801 Davy moved from the politically radical Medical Pneumatic Institution in Bristol to the much staider Royal Institution in London, in the course of which he changed his patronage from Beddoes to Banks. Although it would seem that Nicholson was never a subscriber of any sort to the Royal Institution, he did join its Committee of Chemistry in June 1801[172] shortly after Davy's arrival, and thereafter for a number of years regularly presented copies of his *Journal*. By this time Davy, apart from one paper and two very short notes, had effectively ceased publishing in *Nicholson's Journal* despite it having contributed significantly to making his national reputation. In part, this was because in 1802 Nicholson had a row with Banks about the publication of papers read to the Royal Society of London in his *Journal*,[173] and Davy would never cross Banks.

What Nicholson had achieved with his *Journal* was to show that there existed a readership and a market for monthly journals devoted to scientific matters, promoting the timely publication of the latest pieces of scientific work. Others took notice of this and sought to copy him with monthlies such as the *Philosophical Magazine* (1798) and (a bit later) *Annals of Philosophy* (1813). However, in the long run the market was unable, at least at that time, to support more than one journal and they were eventually merged into the *Philosophical Magazine*.

Although there is little discussion of *Nicholson's Journal* in this memoir, it nevertheless evokes the rich and diverse culture of London science in which Nicholson was located and made his significant scientific contributions.

171. Humphry Davy to Davies Giddy, 20 October 1800, Paris, Vol. 1, pp. 108–11.
172. RI MS MM, 29 June 1801, Vol. 2, p. 197.
173. Watts, pp. 18–122.

I used to write a page or two perhaps in half a year, and I remember laughing heartily at the celebrated experimentalist Nicholson who told me that in twenty years he had written as much as would make three hundred octavo volumes.

— William Hazlitt, *Table-talk: or Original Essays*,
London: J. Warren, 1821

APPENDIX A

Published works by William Nicholson

Books

The British Encyclopedia, or Dictionary of Arts and Sciences: Comprising an Accurate and Popular View of the Present Improved State of Human Knowledge, William Nicholson, 6 volumes, London: Longman, Hurst, Rees and Orme, 1809

A Dictionary of Chemistry: Exhibiting the Present State of the Theory and Practice of That Science, Its Application to Natural Philosophy, the Processes of Manufactures, Metallurgy, and Numerous Other Arts Dependent on the Properties and Habitudes of Bodies, in the Mineral, Vegetable, and Animal Kingdoms: with a Considerable Number of Tables, Expressing the Elective Attractions, Specific Gravities, Comparative Heats, Component Parts, Combinations, and Other Affections of the Objects of Chemical Research, 2 volumes, William Nicholson, London: G.G.J. Robinson and J. Robinson, 1795

A Dictionary of Practical and Theoretical Chemistry: With Its Application of the Arts and Manufactures and to the Explanation of the Phenomena of Nature, William Nicholson, London: printed for Richard Phillips by Richard Taylor and Co., 1808

First Principles of Chemistry, William Nicholson, 1st edn, London: G.G.J. Robinson and J. Robinson, 1790; 2nd edn, 1792; 3rd edn, 1796

An Introduction to Natural Philosophy, William Nicholson, London: J. Johnson, 2 volumes, 1st edn, 1782; 2nd edn, 1787; 3rd edn, 1790; 4th edn, 1796; 5th edn, 1805

The Navigator's Assistant, Containing the Theory and Practice of Navigation, William Nicholson, London: T. Longman, T. Cadell and J. Sewell, 1784

Contributions

Aikin, J., Enfield, W., Nicholson, W., Morgan, T. and Johnston, W., *General Biography; or Lives Critical and Historical, of the Most Eminent Persons of All Ages, Countries, Conditions, and Professions, Arranged According to Alphabetical Order*, Vols 2 and 3, London: G.G.J. Robinson and J. Robinson, 1801 and 1802

Holcroft, Thomas, *Alwyn: or the Gentleman Comedian in Two Volumes*, with contributions by William Nicholson, London: Fielding and Walker, 1780

Holcroft, Thomas, *Duplicity: A Comedy, in Five Acts*, prologue by William Nicholson, 1st and 2nd edns, London: G. Robinson, 1781; 3rd edn, 1782

Ralph, James, with additional information by William Nicholson, *A Critical Review of the Public Buildings, Statues, and Ornaments, in and about London and Westminster*, rev. edn, London: J. Wallis, 1783

Journals

The General Review of British and Foreign Literature, William Nicholson (ed.), Vol. 1, London: D. N. Shury, 1806

A Journal of Natural Philosophy, Chemistry and the Arts, William Nicholson (ed.), 36 volumes (1797–1813): available online at *www.nicholsonsjournal.co.uk*

Series 1, Vols 1–5 (London: G.G.J. Robinson and J. Robinson, 1797–1801); Series 2, Vols 1–7 (1802–4)

Series 2, Vols 8–14 (London: W. Stratford, 1804–6)

Series 2, Vol. 15 (London: N. Shury, 1806)

Series 2, Vols 16–17 (London, J. Stratford, 1807)

Series 2, Vol. 18 (London: W. Stratford, 1807)

Series 2, Vols 19–32 (London, J. Stratford, 1808–12)

Series 2, Vols 33–6 (London: G. Sidney, 1812–13)

Papers

An Abstract of Such Acts of Parliament as Are Now in Force, for Preventing the Exportation of Wool and Other Commodities, Tools, and Implements Used in the Manufactures Thereof: and Also for Preventing the Seducing of Artists into Foreign Parts, [William Nicholson] (Secretary), Chamber of Manufacturers of Great Britain, London, 1785

'A Description of a New Instrument for Measuring the Specific Gravities of Bodies', William Nicholson in a letter to Mr J.H. Magellan, *Memoirs of the Manchester Literary and Philosophical Society*, Warrington, 1785, pp. 370–80

'A Description of an Instrument Which, by the Turning of a Winch, Produces the Two States of Electricity Without Friction or Communication with the Earth. Communicated by Sir Joseph Banks', William Nicholson, *Philosophical Transactions of the Royal Society of London*, 1788, pp. 403–7

'Experiments and Observations on Electricity. Communicated by Sir Joseph Banks', William Nicholson, *Philosophical Transactions of the Royal Society of London*, 1789, Vol. 79, pp. 265–88

A Letter to the Incorporated Company of Proprietors of the Portsea-Island Water-Works, Occasioned by an Application Lately Made to Them by the Assigns, Under an Act of the 14th Year of George III for Conveying Water from Farlington, [William Nicholson], London, 1810

Observations on a Bill, for Explaining, Amending, and Reducing into One Act the Several Laws Now in Being . . . for Preventing the Exportation of Live Sheep, Wool, and Other Commodities, William Nicholson, London, 1787

'Papers in Mechanicks "Letter on the Subject of Mr Hardy's Counterbalance"', William Nicholson, G. Smart, G. Gilpin, W. Heather, R. Salmon, P. Herbert, C. Le Caan, J. Davis, A. Flint, J. Hawkins, J. Antis, W. Hardy and J. Prior, *Transactions of the Society, Instituted at London, for the Encouragement of Arts, Manufactures, and Commerce*, Vol. 23, 1805, pp. 387–90

'The Principles and Illustration of an Advantageous Method of Arranging the Differences of Logarithms, on Lines Graduated for the Purpose of Computation. Communicated by Sir Joseph Banks', William Nicholson, *Philosophical Transactions of the Royal Society of London*, 1787, Vol. 77, pp. 246–52

A Summary Abstract of the Evidence Given by the Manufacturers Before the Committee of the House of Lords of Great Britain Against the Irish Propositions: Being a Continuation of the Minutes of Evidence Given Before the House of Commons, William Nicholson (Secretary), Chamber of Manufacturers of Great Britain, 1785 (HL/PO/JO/10/7/705, Houses of Parliament)

Nicholson also published his own scientific papers in *A Journal of Natural Philosophy, Chemistry and the Arts*. A list of sixty-two papers can be found in the *Royal Society Catalogue of Scientific Papers IV*, pp. 610–612

Translations

Benyowsky, Maurice Auguste, Count de Benyowsky, *Memoirs and Travels of Mauritius Augustus Count De Benyowsky: Magnate of the Kingdom of Hungary and Poland, One of the Chiefs of the Confederation of Poland & C., &C.* 'Consisting of his military operations in Poland, his exile in Kamchatka, his escape and voyage from that peninsula through the northern Pacific ocean, touching at Japan and Formosa, to Canton in China, with an account of the French settlement he was appointed to form upon the island of Madagascar.' Translated by William Nicholson, 1st edn, 2 volumes, London: G.G.J. Robinson and J. Robinson, 1790

Chaptal, Jean-Antoine-Claude, *Chemistry Applied to Arts and Manufactures*, translated by William Nicholson, 4 volumes, printed for R. Phillips by J. Ardland, London, 1807

Chaptal, Jean-Antoine-Claude, *Elements of Chemistry*, translated by William Nicholson, 3 volumes, London: G.G.J. Robinson and J. Robinson, 1791

Charmes, Claude Pajot des, *The Art of Bleaching Piece-goods, Cottons, and Threads, of Every Description, Rendered more Easy and General by Means of the Oxygenated Muriatic Acid; and with the Method of Rendering Painted or Printed Goods Perfectly White or Colourless. to Which Are Added the Most Certain Methods of Bleaching Silk and Wool; and the Discoveries Made by the Author in the Art of Bleaching Paper*, translated by William Nicholson, 2 volumes, London: G.G.J. Robinson and J. Robinson, 1799

Fourcroy, Antoine-François de, *Elements of Natural History, and of Chemistry: Being the Second Edition of the Elementary Lectures on These Sciences*, 'first published in 1782, and now greatly enlarged and improved by the author', 4 volumes, translated by William Nicholson, London: G.G.J. Robinson and J. Robinson, 1788

Fourcroy, Antoine-François de, *A General System of Chemical Knowledge and Its Application to the Phenomena of Nature and Art*, 11 volumes, translated by William Nicholson, London: Cadell and Davies, 1804

Fourcroy, Antoine-François de, *Supplement to the Elements of Natural History and of Chemistry, of M. De Fourcroy, Doctor of the Faculty Of Medicine, & C. Carefully Extracted from the Edition of 1789, and Adapted to the English, by the Translator of That Work*, translated by William Nicholson, London: G.G.J. Robinson and J. Robinson, 1789

Fourcroy, Antoine-François de, *Synoptic Tables of Chemistry*, translated by William Nicholson, London: R. Noble, 1801

Kirwan, Richard, *An Essay on Phlogiston, and the Constitution of Acids: A New Edition by R. Kirwan . . . to Which Are Added Notes Exhibiting and Defending the Antiphlogistic Theory; and Annexed to the French Edition of This Work; by Messrs de Morveau, Lavoisier, de la Place, Monge, Berthollet, and de Fourcroy*, translated and with notes by William Nicholson, 1st edn, J. Davis for P. Elmsly, London, 1787; 2nd edn, London: J. Johnson, 1789

Maistre de La Tour, M, *History of Hyder Shah, Alias Hyder Ali Khan Bahadur, or New Memoirs Concerning the East Indies with Historical Notes*, translated by William Nicholson, London: J. Johnson, 1784

Venturi, J.B., *Experimental Enquiries Concerning the Principle of the Lateral Communication of Motion in Fluids Applied to the Explanation of Various Hydraulic Phenomena*, translated by William Nicholson, London: J. Taylor at the Architectural Library, 1799

APPENDIX B

Inventions and patents by William Nicholson

Nicholson's hydrometer (1784)

William Nicholson, 'A description of a new instrument for measuring the specific gravities of bodies' in a letter to Mr J. H Magellan, *Memoirs of the Manchester Literary and Philosophical Society*, London: Warrington, 1785, pp. 370–80

Sliding scale rule for computing longitude (1786)

MSS RGO 14/45 – RGO 14/68, *Papers of the Board of Longitude*. Courtesy of University of Cambridge, Digital Library

Scale rule designs (1787)

William Nicholson, 'The Principles and Illustration of an Advantageous Method of Arranging the Differences of Logarithms, on Lines Graduated for the Purpose of Computation', Communicated by Sir Joseph Banks, Bart. P. R. S., Phil. Trans. R. Soc London, January 1, 1787 77 246–252

Revolving doubler (1787)

William Nicholson, 'A Description of an Instrument Which, by the Turning of a Winch, Produces the Two States of Electricity Without Friction or Communication with the Earth', *Royal Society of London, Philosophical Transactions*, No. 78, London, 1788

Cylindrical printing machine (1790)

Patent GB1748 of 1790 to William Nicholson of New North Street, Red Lyon Square, Middlesex: 'A Machine or Instrument on a New Construction for the Purpose of Printing on Paper, Linen, Cotton, Woollen and Other Articles in a More Neat, Cheap and Accurate Manner Than Is Effected by the Machines Now in Use'

Gravity escapement clock (1797)

A satinwood cased eight-day bracket timepiece with gravity escapement, with round silvered-metal dial with centre-seconds, TRAIN-COUNT, Gt wheel 180 2nd wheel 144/12 3rd wheel 144/12 4th wheel 60/12 Escape wheel 10/10 Motion work, 2nd whl pinion 24 driving Min whl pinion 48 driven Minute wheel 120 Minute pinion 32 Hour wheel 80 Canon pinion 25'. Described as 'an interesting example of a rather unassuming case which in reality conceals a movement of a most unusual and interesting design'.[174]

Scale rule designs (1797)

William Nicholson, 'A method of disposing GUNTER'S line of numbers, by which the divisions are enlarged, and other advantages obtained', Nicholson's *Journal*, Vol. I, 1797, p. 375

File manufacturing machine (1802)

Patent GB 2641 of 1802 to William Nicholson of Soho Square, Middlesex: 'Certain Machinery for the Better and More Expeditious Manufacturing of Files'

Improvements in the Application of Steam (1806)

Patent GB 2990 of 1806 to William Nicholson of Soho Square, Middlesex: 'Various Improvements in the Application of Steam to Useful Purposes, and in the Apparatus Required to Effect the Same'

Improvements to Wheel Carriages (1812)

Patent GB 3514 of 1812 to William Nicholson of Bloomsbury Square, Middlesex: 'Certain Improvements in the Method of Manner of Supporting or Suspending the Bodies of Principal Parts of Wheel Carriages.' No specification was attached to this application

---

174. David Thompson, *Clocks*, London: British Museum Press, 2004.

APPENDIX C

Members, as listed in 'Book A' of the Minutes of the Coffee House Philosophical Society, 1780–7

This list of thirty-five names provided by Nicholson is not complete, as Nicholson was not a member from the date of the society's formation. Gerard L'E. Turner provides a comprehensive analysis of fifty-five known members of the society including their attendance record in *Discussing Chemistry and Steam*, Oxford University Press, Oxford, 2002.

ODNB = profile in Online Dictionary of National Biography
FRS = Fellow of the Royal Society
Lunar = Member of the Lunar Society

Title, First name, Last name (BD)	Address given	ODNB	FRS	Lunar	Description
Alexander Aubert (1730–1805)	Austin Friars, 26	√	√	—	Astronomer and merchant
William Babington (1756–1833)		√	√	—	Physician and geologist
Andrew Blackhall	Thavies Inn, Holborn	—	—	—	Physician
Dr William Cleghorn (1754–83)	Haymarket, 11	—	—	—	Physician
Dr John Cooke (c.1756–1838)		√	√	—	Physician
Dr Adair Crawford (1748–95)	Lambs Conduit Street, 48	√	√	—	Physician and chemist
Jean-Hyacinth de Magellan (1722–90)	Nevilles Court, 12	√	√	—	Agent for scientific instruments and horologist
Major Valentine Gardiner (1775–1803)		—	—	—	Balloon enthusiast
Dr William Hamilton (1758–1807)		—	—	—	Physician
James Horsfall (d.1785)	Inner Temple	—	√	—	Mathematician, librarian

Title, First name, Last name (BD)	Address given	ODNB	FRS	Lunar	Description
Dr John Hunter (c.1754–1809)		√	√	—	Physician
Dr Charles Hutton (1737–1823)		√	√	—	Mathematician
William Jones (1746–94)	Inner Temple	√	√	—	Barrister and orientalist
Dr William Keir (1752–83)	Adelphi	—	—	—	Physician
Richard Kirwan (1733–1812)	Newman Street, 11	√	√	—	Chemist, minerologist, meterorologist
Dr William Lister (1756–1830)		—	—	—	Physician
Patrick Miller (1731–1815)	Sackville Street, 17	√	—	—	Banker and inventor
Edward Nairne (1726–1806)	Cornhill, 20	√	√	—	Scientific instrument maker
William Nicholson (1753–1815)		√	—	—	Inventor, publisher, patent agent
Dr George Pearson (1751–1828)		√	√	—	Physician and chemist
Dr Thomas Percival (1740–1804)		√	√	√	Physician
Dr Charles William Quin (1755–1818)	Haymarket, 11	—	—	—	Physician
Dr John Sims (1749–1831)	Paternoster Row, 11	√	√	—	Physician and botanist
Benjamin Vaughan (1751–1835)	Dunster Court, Mincing Lane	√	—	—	Agriculturalist and political reformer
Adam Walker (c.1731–1821)	George Street, Hanover Square	√	—	—	Inventor and lecturer
Dr William Charles Wells (1757–1817)	Salisbury Court	√	√	—	Physician

Title, First name, Last name (BD)	Address given	ODNB	FRS	Lunar	Description
John Whitehurst (1713–88)	Bolt Court, 4 Fleet Street	√	√	√	Maker of scientific instruments and horologist
Dr John Watkinson (1742–83)	Crutched Friars, 22	—	—	—	Physician
Josiah Wedgwood (1730–95)	Etruria	√	√	√	Ceramicist and successful entrepreneur – attended eight times

Honorary members

Title, First name, Last name (BD)	Address given	ODNB	FRS	Lunar	Description
Dr Matthew Boulton (1728–1809)	Birmingham	√	√	√	Engineer and successful entrepreneur – never attended. Active member of General Chamber of Manufacturers with Wedgwood and Nicholson
Richard Bright (1754–1840)	Bristol	—	—	—	Merchant banker – attended only once
James Keir (1735–1820)	Birmingham	√	√	√	Chemist and manufacturer – never attended but met Nicholson in 1785 when taking evidence for the General Chamber of Manufacturers
Dr Richard Price (1723–91)	Newington Green	√	—	—	Preacher and author – never attended
Revd Dr Joseph Priestley (1733–1804)	Birmingham	√	√	√	Preacher, scientist and author – only attended once
James Watt (1736–1819)	Birmingham	√	√	√	Engineer and successful entrepreneur – never attended

APPENDIX D

The Committee of the Society for the Improvement of Naval Architecture, 1791

	First name, Last name (BD)	ODNB	Description
President	HRH Duke of Clarence, William (1765–1837)	√	William IV, 'the Sailor King' – he commissioned the first steam warship
Vice-president	Earl Stanhope, Charles (1753–1816)	√	Politician and scientist who patented several inventions in connection with ships
Vice-president	Earl of Leicester, George Townshend (1753–1811)	√	Politician and antiquary
Vice-president	Earl of Uxbridge, Henry Paget (1768–1854)	—	Army officer and politician
Vice-president	Lord Rawdon, Francis Rawdon-Hastings (1754–1826)	√	Military officer and politician, Governor-General of India from 1813 to 1823
Vice-president	Lord Mulgrave, Constantine John Phipps (1744–92)	√	Naval officer and politician
Vice-president / Committee	Sir John Borlase Warren (1753–1822)	√	Co-founder of society; naval officer and diplomat
Vice-president / Committee	Sir Joseph Banks (1743–1820)	√	Naturalist and long-serving president of the Royal Society
Vice-president	Sir Charles Middleton (1726–1813)	√	Naval officer and abolitionist
Committee	Sir Charles Henry Knowles (1754–1831)	√	Naval officer
Committee	Alexander Aubert (1730–1805)	√	Astronomer and member of the philosophical coffee society with Nicholson
Committee	Daniel Braithwaite	—	Co-owner of the *European Magazine*

	First name, Last name (BD)	ODNB	Description
Committee	John Brent (1729–1812)	—	Surveyor and shipbuilder
Committee	Daniel Brent (1764–1834)	—	Shipbuilder (son of John Brent)
Committee	Revd John De Veil	—	
Committee	John Fiott	—	Ship owner/merchant
Committee	William Fraser (d.1818)	—	Captain, later knighted
Committee	John Hallett (c.1772–94)	—	Midshipman on HMS *Bounty*
Committee	Dr Charles Hutton (1737–1823)	√	Mathematician
Committee	Capt. William Lockyer	—	Captain, sailed with Horatio Nelson
Committee/ Secretary	Revd Thomas Martyn (1735–1825)	√	Co-founder of society; Professor of Botany at Cambridge University
Committee	William Nicholson (1753–1815)	√	Inventor, publisher, patent agent
Committee	John Randall (1755–1802)	√	Shipbuilder
Committee	Isaac Rogers (1754–1839)	√	Watchmaker and merchant
Committee	John Sewell (c.1734–1802)	—	Co-founder of society; Co-owner of the *European Magazine*
Committee	Revd Anthony Shepherd (c.1721–96)	√	Plumian chair of Astronomy and Experimental Philosophy at University of Cambridge; the Shepherd Islands were named after him by Captain Cook
Committee	Marmaduke Stalkartt (c.1750–1805)	√	Naval architect and shipbuilder
Committee	William Tennant	—	Lived in Dover Street

Note: The society had an extensive membership that included other associates of William Nicholson including Colonel Mark Beaufoy, FRS, John Debrett (d.1822), Charles Francis Greville (1749–1809) and Nevil Maskelyne (1732–1811).

INDEX